Oracle Utilities

*Using Hidden Programs, Import/Export, SQL*loader, Oradebug, Dbverify, Tkprof and More*

Dave Moore

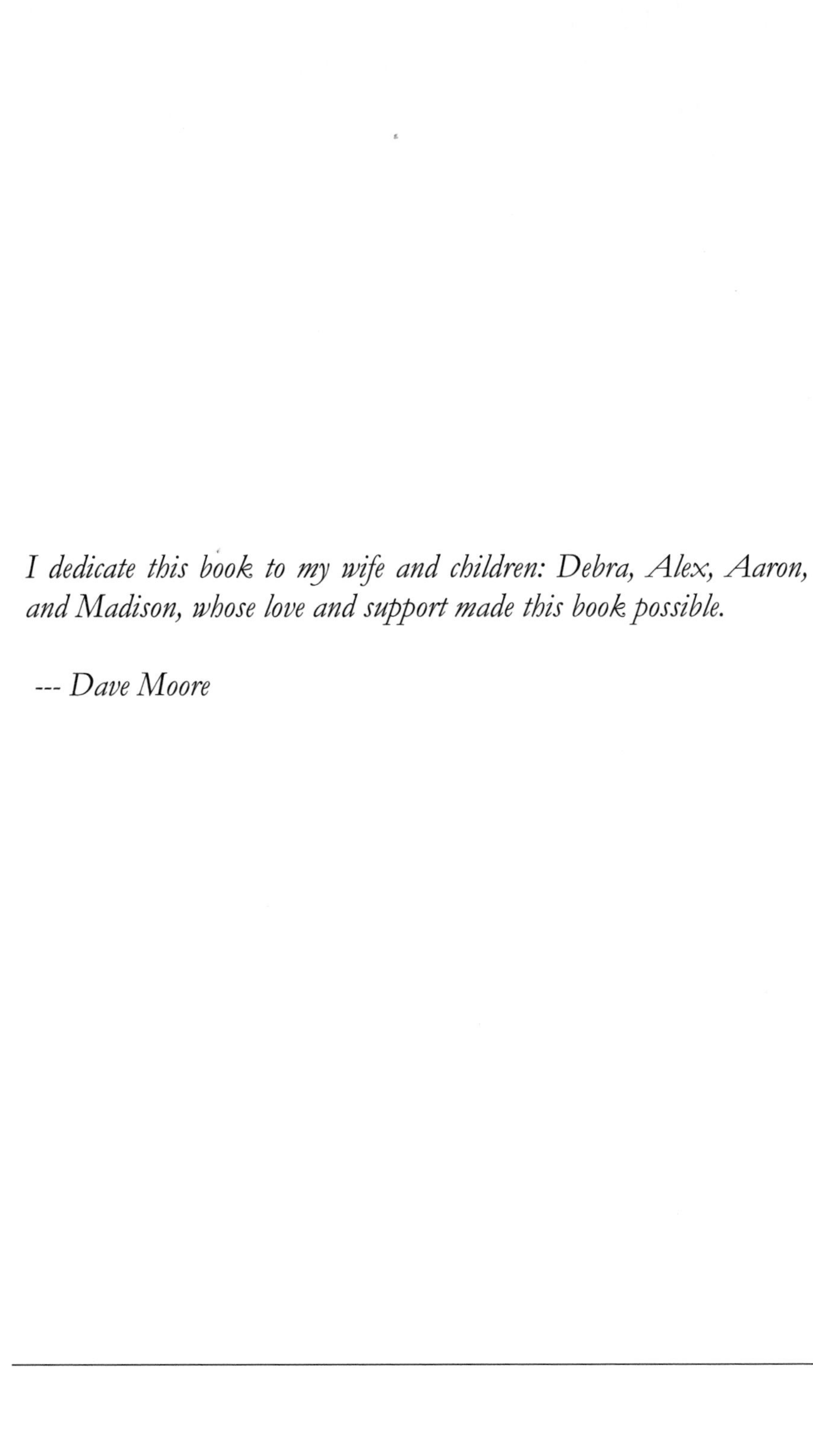

I dedicate this book to my wife and children: Debra, Alex, Aaron, and Madison, whose love and support made this book possible.

--- Dave Moore

Oracle Utilities

*Using Hidden Programs, Import/Export, SQL*loader, Oradebug, Dbverify, Tkprof and More*

By Dave Moore

Printed in the United States of America.

Published by Rampant TechPress, Kittrell, North Carolina, USA

Oracle In-Focus Series: Book #6

Series Editor: Don Burleson

Editors: Robert Strickland, John Lavender, and Linda Webb

Production Editor: Teri Wade

Cover Design: Bryan Hoff

Printing History:

June 2003 for First Edition

ISBN: 0-9727513-5-1

Library of Congress Control Number: 2003105335

Table of Contents

Using the Online Code Depot

Your purchase of this book provides you with complete access to the online code depot that contains the sample tests and answers.

Within the text, all code depot listing are denoted with a diskette icon as follows:

sample_script.sql

All of the job questions in this book are located at the following URL:

rampant.cc/util.htm

All of the sample tests in this book will be available for download in a zip format, ready to load and use on your database.

If you need technical assistance in downloading or accessing the scripts, please contact Rampant TechPress at info@rampant.cc.

Conventions Used in this Book

It is critical for any technical publication to follow rigorous standards and employ consistent punctuation conventions to make the text easy to read.

However, this is not an easy task. Within Oracle there are many types of notation that can confuse a reader. Some Oracle utilities such as STATSPACK are always spelled in CAPITAL letters, while Oracle parameters and procedures have varying naming conventions in the Oracle documentation. It is also important to remember that many Oracle commands are case sensitive, and are always left in their original executable form, and never altered with italics or capitalization.

Hence, all Rampant TechPress books follow these conventions:

Parameters - All Oracle parameters will be *lowercase italics.* Exceptions to this rule will be parameter arguments that are commonly capitalized (KEEP pool, TKPROF); those will be left in ALL CAPS.

Variables – All PL/SQL program variables and arguments will also remain in lowercase italics (*dbms_job, dbms_utility*).

Tables & dictionary objects – All data dictionary objects are referenced in lowercase italics (*dba_indexes, v$sql*). This includes all v$ and x$ views (*x$kcbcbh, v$parameter*) and dictionary views (*dba_tables, user_indexes*).

SQL – All SQL is formatted for easy use in the code depot, and all SQL is displayed in lowercase. The main SQL terms (select, from, where, group by, order by, having) will always appear on a separate line.

Programs & Products – All products and programs that are known to the author are capitalized according the vendor specifications (IBM, DBXray, etc). All names known to Rampant TechPress to be trademark names appear in this text as initial caps. References to UNIX are always made in uppercase.

Acknowledgements

First and foremost, this book would not be possible without the assistance of Don Burleson. Don convinced me to put my life on hold to share some of my Oracle knowledge with the rest of the world, and I thank him for that.

Thanks to John Lavender at Rampant TechPress for brilliantly managing this project and tolerating my constant, last-minute updates.

I also want to thank other members of the Rampant staff, especially Bob Strickland for cleaning-up my bad grammar, Linda Webb for copyediting, and Teri Wade for her superb page formatting.

To my colleagues at BMC Software who have assisted me along the way, I owe my gratitude, not only for their assistance with this book, but also for providing such a stimulating environment that we are lucky enough to call "work".

These include Chris Breazeal, Chet Henry, Mark Wright, Lenny Blumberg, Marc Melancon, Andy Galindo, Mark Bennett, and Rusty Bullerman. In particular, I owe many thanks to Julian Dyke for his relentless technical reviews.

I also want to thank Carlos Sierra and others at Oracle Metalink supports, who have graciously answered my many questions.

Thanks to Hugh Morrow, the provider of the artwork in this book. There simply is no better visual designer/graphical artist than Hugh.

Finally, I want to acknowledge my mentor Dave Ensor, who has taught me more about Oracle than I could have ever imagined.

With my sincerest thanks,

Dave Moore

Preface

Most Oracle books on the market today adopt a top-down approach, based on a general theme and title – "Oracle Performance Tuning" or "Oracle PL/SQL", to name a few.

This book takes a completely opposite approach. It starts with the available Oracle utilities and describes their function and how they can be used.

Simply put, some are hidden gems, while others aren't productive at all. There are some very useful utilities that most people don't know about. They exist in every Oracle installation and, at most sites just sit idle.

If you want to become familiar with all of the utilities that Oracle provides as part of the base installation, this book is for you. This book lists the utilities and provides a method for discovering utilities in future releases of Oracle.

This book explains many of the utilities in detail – how they can be used, when to use them, and how they can be optimized. Finally, scripts are provided that utilize or enhance the utilities discussed.

There are three things I want this book to accomplish. First, I want to share the knowledge of the subject matter that I've gained after working with Oracle for many years. As a person who writes software for DBAs, I want to share with you some of what I know.

My second goal is to provide useful scripts that can be utilized immediately.

Finally, this is not a book on Oracle theory. Instead, the focus is on practical solutions, complimented by SQL scripts and code.

Chapter 1

Scripts Used in this Book

Three languages are employed throughout this book to provide useful scripts. The language of choice is used to explain certain utilities even though it can be done in any language. The reader should be able to easily transfer the knowledge in the examples from one language to another.

PL/SQL – Most of the DBMS-supplied packages are detailed using the PL/SQL scripts provided in this book. These include anonymous PL/SQL blocks, as well as stored procedures or packages. This book assumes that the reader knows basic PL/SQL, or will seek the resources needed.

Java – Java is used for any examples that require client side programming. The Java examples provided can be run on Windows, UNIX , or Linux without modification – the true benefit of Java. Some utilities discussed in this book are Java-based utilities only; therefore Java is the only option. This book assumes that the reader knows basic Java, or will seek the resources needed.

Korn Shell - For those utilities that are only available on non-Windows platforms, *ksh* scripts are used where appropriate. The *ksh* scripts provided in the book are very basic and small. Just enough *ksh* and *awk* is used to get the job done, providing a useful script that can be enhanced for particular environments. This assumes that the reader knows the basics of shell scripting, or will seek the resources needed.

Environment Setup and Configuration

The environments that were used to test the scripts provided in this book are described below. The 9i database was the focus for all examples, although they were also tested in version 8.1.

Database and Platforms

- Oracle 9.2.0.1.0 on Windows XP 2002 on Pentium 4 1.70 GHz
- Oracle 9.2.0.1.0 on SunOS 5.8 Sun4u Sparc SUNW, Ultra-80

Java

The Java Software Development Kit (SDK) was used to create and execute the Java programs listed in this book. This software can be downloaded from http://java.sun.com. The version of the Java SDK used with the code in this book was 1.3.1_01. All sources should work with that version of the SDK or any later version. The java *–version* command can be used to determine what version of the SDK is currently installed:

```
C:\> java -version
java version "1.3.1_01"
Java(TM) 2 Runtime Environment, Standard Edition (build 1.3.1_01)
Java HotSpot(TM) Client VM (build 1.3.1_01, mixed mode)
```

The Java examples can be compiled using the compiler supplied with the SDK. Any dependent JAR or class files must be present in the CLASSPATH in order for the Java code to successfully compile and execute.

```
C:\>javac ConnectionTest.java
```

The java programs can be executed by specifying the java keyword followed by the class name:

```
C:\>java ConnectionTest
```

JDBC Driver

Most of the Java programs in this book require the JDBC Driver. These examples used the Oracle Thin JDBC Driver version 9.2.0.1, available for download from http://technet.oracle.com.

However, any version of the JDBC Driver will work, provided that it is at least the version level of the database you are trying to access. The 9.2.0.1 version of the driver can access version 8.1 of the database, but not vice-versa.

Once the JDBC driver is installed, the path to the JAR file must be included in the *classpath* environment variable as mentioned above.

Now that we have covered the scripts used in this book, let's get started with a definition of the Oracle utilities.

Chapter 2

Oracle Utilities Defined

This chapter provides the definition of a utility. The actual utilities are listed, as well as a discovery mechanism that will allow anyone to find them in future releases of Oracle.

Due to the complexity of most utilities, they cannot all be discussed in great detail. The rest of the book will explore the most useful utilities. This chapter will only provide the complete lists for the different Oracle versions.

Definition of a Utility

Webster's Dictionary© defines a utility as the following:

- The quality or condition of being useful; a useful article or device.

This book extends this definition into the Oracle world. Tools are supplied with Oracle that can be very useful for DBAs, developers, and system administrators to maintain or enhance the Oracle product. For this reason, they will be known as "Oracle Utilities" in what follows.

A utility is something that is useful in a way that helps you do your job. It could be an operating system executable file, a Windows bat file, a

UNIX shell script, an Oracle supplied package, or a feature of an existing tool that is not widely known.

What is a Hidden Utility?

A hidden utility is not one whose file is physically hidden in the operating system. In fact, it may not be an executable, but instead a PL/SQL source or part of another utility. A hidden utility is one that is rarely revealed and its existence is unknown to most Oracle professionals. Hidden utilities are either undocumented or documentation is difficult to find.

Some executables are not supplied as part of the base Oracle installation. By default, some PL/SQL packages do not exist in the database, although the code to load them exists in the operating system. Other PL/SQL packages are only available via an Oracle MetaLink (Trace Analyzer). Also, certain PL/SQL packages are only accessible to the SYS user by default (*dbms_system*) in some Oracle versions.

While some utilities are included for reasons known only to Oracle Corporation, they are indeed present in the Oracle environment and can be used to solve specific problems.

Utility Locations

The main directories of interest regarding Oracle utilities are the following:

- ***$ORACLE_HOME/bin*** –This contains the binary executables used by the Oracle server. Most of the tools discussed in this book reside here.

- ***$ORACLE_HOME/plsql/demo*** – This contains a useful collection of SQL scripts related to many utilities, including *dbms_profiler*.

- ***$ORACLE_HOME/rdbms/admin*** – This contains many SQL scripts used for creating PL/SQL packages and their required environments.

- ***$ORACLE_HOME/sqlplus/admin*** – This contains scripts used with *autotrace* and other utilities.

- ***$ORACLE_HOME/otrace/admin*** – This is the administration directory for the Oracle Trace diagnostic tool.

- ***$ORACLE_HOME/otrace/sysman*** – This is used by utilities such as oemctl and the Oracle Management Server (OMS).

- ***$ORACLE_HOME/otrace/lib*** – This contains facility files used with the *oerr* utility.

Code Depot Keyword	**fawn**

Given the obscure location of many utilities, we need to learn how to find them. Which utilities exist? Which ones are new?

Methods of Discovery

Although many utilities are documented here, the ability to "discover" them is important in order to know which ones exist. This ability can be transferred with each new release of the database, revealing the presence of new utilities that may or may not be useful.

It typically takes months or even years to become familiar with the key features of a new database version. It takes time for the features to become well-known and the same applies to utilities.

For example, the most popular technical sessions at Oracle World concern TKPROF, even though the utility has existed for many years. There is no need to wait for complete documentation, these utilities can be discovered and applied by the individual. Once we know they exist, they can be investigated and their potential benefits can be realized.

Package Discovery

Fortunately, the PL/SQL packages that are installed in the database are the easiest utilities to find. To reveal the new packages, a database link must be created within the version of Oracle that contains the packages. The database link should point to a prior version of Oracle. This allows a query to be executed to determine the differences between the two databases.

For example, the following query, through a database link, displays the packages that were added in Oracle version 9.2, as compared to 8.1.7.3.

```
select object_name
   from dba_objects
   where owner       = 'SYS'
    and object_type = 'PACKAGE BODY'
    minus
    select object_name
      from  dba_objects@ORCL8173
         where owner       = 'SYS'
         and object_type = 'PACKAGE BODY';
```

This query simply displays all of the package bodies owned by SYS that exist in 9.2 but not in 8.1.7.3. The same query can be executed to compare packages in any two databases, provided that the database link object exists to connect the two instances.

Binary Discovery

Discovering new binary executables is slightly more involved than discovering database objects. It entails comparing two directories in the operating system and ignoring the duplicates. The *dircmp* command in UNIX can be used for this procedure because it compares two directories and reports the differences – exactly what we want.

```
dircmp -s <directory 1> <directory 2>
```

The *–s* option of the *dircmp* command tells UNIX to eliminate the matches from the output.

Unfortunately, no operating system command exists on Windows to perform such a comparison. It is also more difficult to access the physical drives on separate Windows machines than UNIX machines. However, the DIR/B DOS command can be used to list the files in a directory and the output can be redirected to a file. The two files can then be compared using any number of tools.

Other Things worth Discovering

The same approach used to discover new PL/SQL packages can be applied to find other useful features in new versions of the database. The following new Oracle features can be easily discovered:

- **Instance Parameters** – New instance parameters can easily be identified with the following query:

```
 select name
   from v$parameter
minus
select name
   from v$parameter@PRIOR_VERSION;
```

- **Obsolete Parameters** – Oracle provides a list of obsolete parameters with each version of the database, beginning in 8.1.5.

```
select name
   from v$obsolete_parameter
minus
select name
   from v$obsolete_parameter@PRIOR_VERSION;
```

- **V$ Views** - New *v$* and *gv$* views are usually an indicator of new functionality in the database. They are listed with the following query:

```
select view_name
   from v$fixed_view_definition
minus
select view_name
   from v$fixed_view_definition@PRIOR_VERSION;
```

- **System Events** – The new system events are also very interesting to DBAs. Some of them offer new tuning features. They can be obtained from the following query:

```
select name
   from v$event_name
minus
select name
   from v$event_name@PRIOR_VERSION;
```

The *@PRIOR_VERSION* contained in each query above represents a database link to another version of Oracle. This designation can be used to find any new characteristic of the database via an SQL statement.

The next section of this book will categorize the PL/SQL and binary utilities according to the version of the database.

Package Utilities

Oracle supplied 34 PL/SQL packages with version 7.3.4 of the database and this grew to an astonishing 287 packages in Oracle 9.2. This increase indicates that the number of new database features being supplied in PL/SQL packages has grown tremendously.

The table below lists the supplied Oracle packages, a brief description, and the version of Oracle that first made it available. Version 7.3.4 is the oldest included in this book, even though the package may have been available before 7.3.4.

Package	Description	First Available
dbms_alert	Asynchronous event notification	(7.3.4)
dbms_application_info	Application registration	(7.3.4)
dbms_apply_adm	Streams Apply Process Administration	9.2
dbms_aq	Advanced Queue Manipulation	8.0
dbms_aqadm	Advanced Queueing Administration	8.0
dbms_aqelm	Advanced Queueing Asynchronous Notification Administration	9.0.1
dbms_capture_adm	Streams Capture Process Administration	9.2
dbms_cdc_publish	Change Data Capture Publishing Routines	9.0.1
dbms_cdc_subscribe	Change Data Capture Subscription Routines	9.0.1

Package	Description	First Available
dbms_cdc_utility	Change Data Capture Utilities	9.0.1
dbms_ddl	DDL functions	(7.3.4)
dbms_debug	Server Side Debugger	(7.3.4)
dbms_defer	User interface to RPC facility	(7.3.4)
dbms_defer_query	Query deferred transactions queue	(7.3.4)
dbms_defer_sys	Manage default replication node lists	(7.3.4)
dbms_describe	Describes stored procedure arguments	(7.3.4)
dbms_distributed_trust_admin	Maintains Trusted Database List	8.0
dbms_drs	Hot Standby	9.0.1
dbms_fga	Fine Grained Auditing	9.0.1
dbms_flashback	Flashback Query	9.0.1
dbms_job	Job Scheduler	(7.3.4)
dbms_lob	LOB Management	8.0
dbms_lock	Interface to Lock Management Services	(7.3.4)
dbms_logmnr	Log Miner	8.1.5
dbms_logmnr_d	Log Miner Dictionary Routines	8.1.5
dbms_logstdby	Logical Standby routines	9.0.1
dbms_metadata	Metadata routines	9.0.1
dbms_mview	Materialized Views	8.1.5
dbms_obfuscation_toolkit	Code Obfuscation	8.1.6
dbms_odci	Extensible Optimizer	9.0.1
dbms_offline_og	Offline instantiation of master groups	(7.3.4)
dbms_offline_snapshot	Offline instantiation of snapshots	8.0
dbms_outln	Stored Outline Administration see OUTLN_PKG	8.1.5

Package	Description	First Available
dbms_outln_edit	Stored Outline Editing see OUTLN_EDIT_PKG	9.0.1
dbms_output	PL/SQL Output Buffer	(7.3.4)
dbms_pipe	Inter-session message pipe	(7.3.4)
dbms_profiler	PL/SQL Performance Profiler	8.1.5
dbms_propagation_adm	Streams Propagation Process Administration	9.2
dbms_random	Random number generator	8.0
dbms_rectifier_diff	Shows differences between two replicated sites see DBMS_REPCAT_SNA	8.0
dbms_redefinition	Table Online Reorgs	9.0.1
dbms_refresh	Refreshes materialized views (snapshots)	(7.3.4)
dbms_repair	Block Corruption	8.1.5
dbms_repcat	Replication Catalog and Environment Administration	(7.3.4)
dbms_repcat_admin	Replication User Administration	9.0.1
dbms_repcat_instantiate	Replication Instantiate Deployment Templates	8.1.5
dbms_repcat_rgt	Replication Refresh Group Templates	8.1.5
dbms_repcat_sna	Shows differences between two replicated sites see DBMS_RECTIFIER_DIFF	8.0
dbms_reputil	Replication utilities	(7.3.4)

Package	Description	First Available
dbms_resource_manager	Plans, Consumer groups, plan directives	8.1.5
dbms_resource_manager_privs	Consumer group privileges	8.1.5
dbms_resumable	Resumable session management	9.0.1
dbms_rls	Row Level Security	8.1.5
dbms_rowid	ROWID manipulation	8.0
dbms_rule	Rule evaluation	8.1.5
dbms_rule_adm	Rule administration	8.1.5
dbms_session	Session Utilities including ALTER Session	(7.3.4)
dbms_snapshot	Snapshots (see DBMS_MVIEW)	(7.3.4)
dbms_space	Segment space info	(7.3.4)
dbms_space_admin	Segment space administration	8.1.5
dbms_sql	Dynamic SQL	(7.3.4)
dbms_stats	Optimizer Statistics	8.1.5
dbms_storage_map	FMON Mapping operations	9.2
dbms_streams	Streams Utilities	9.2
dbms_streams_adm	Streams Administration	9.2
dbms_summary	Summary Advisor	8.1.5
dbms_system	System utilities	(7.3.4)
dbms_support	Support (Tracing) Routines	8.0.6
dbms_trace	PL/SQL Tracing	8.1.5
dbms_transaction	Transaction control statements	(7.3.4)
dbms_transform	Advanced Queueing message format transformations	9.0.1
dbms_tts	Transportable Tablespaces	8.1.5
dbms_utility	Miscellaneous utility routines	(7.3.4)
dbms_wm	Workspace Manager	9.2

Package	Description	First Available
dbms_xdb	XML Database Resource Management	9.2
dbms_xdbt	XDB ContextIndex routines	9.2
dbms_xdb_version	XDB Versioning routines	9.2
dbms_xmldom	XML DOM Parser	9.2
dbms_xmlgen	XML generation	9.0.1
dbms_xmlparser	Access contents and structure of XML documents	9.2
dbms_xmlquery	Database to XML routines (use DBMS_XMLGEN instead)	8.1.7
dbms_xmlsave	Save XML to Database routines	8.1.7
dbms_xmlschema	XML Schema Manipulation	9.2
dbms_xplan	Explain Plan	9.2
dbms_xslprocessor	XSL Processor routines (Stylesheets)	9.2
htf	Web Agent Hypertext Functions	8.1.7
htp	Web Agent Hypertext Print Routines	8.1.7
outln_edit_pkg	Stored Outline Editing Routines see DBMS_OUTLN_EDIT	9.0.1
outln_pkg	Stored Outlines see DBMS_OUTLN	8.1.5
owa	Oracle Web Agent Interface Procedures	8.1.7
owa_cache	Web Agent Content Caching Functions	8.1.7
owa_cookie	Web Agent Cookie Manipulation Functions	8.1.7
owa_custom	Web Agent Customization Functions	8.1.7

Package	**Description**	**First Available**
owa_image	Web Agent Image Handling Functions	8.1.7
owa_opt_lock	Web Agent Optimistic Locking Functions	8.1.7
owa_pattern	Web Agent String Manipulation Functions	8.1.7
owa_sec	WebServer Security Functions	8.1.7
owa_text	WebServer Text Handling Functions	8.1.7
owa_util	WebServer Utility Functions	8.1.7
standard	Built-in functions	(7.3.4)
urifactory	URI Manipulation Functions	9.0.1
utl_coll	Collection Locators	8.1.5
utl_encode	Encodes raw data	9.0.1
utl_file	External File Access	(7.3.4)
utl_gdk	Globalization Development Kit	9.2
utl_http	HTTP access from PL/SQL	(7.3.4)
utl_inaddr	Internet address API	8.1.7
utl_raw	SQL functions for RAW datatypes	(7.3.4)
utl_ref	Access to objects via references	8.0
utl_smtp	SMTP E-Mail Interface Library	8.1.7
utl_tcp	TCP/IP Interface Library	8.1.7
utl_url	Escape mechanism for URL characters	9.0.1
utl_xml	XML/XSL Utility Library	9.0.1

Table 2.1 - The supplied Oracle packages.

UNIX Utilities and Shell Scripts

The table below lists the UNIX binaries provided in Oracle 9.2, a brief description, and the version of Oracle that first made it available.

Binary	**Description**	**First Available**
adapters	Installed Network Adapters	(7.3.4)
agentctl	Agent Control Utility	9.0.1
agtctl	Agent Control Utility	8.1.5
bulkmodify	Oracle Internet Directory bulk modify	8.1.6
cmadmin	Connection Manager Administrator	8.1.6
cmctl	Connection Manager Control Utility	8.1.6
cmgw	Connection Manager Gateway	8.1.6
coraenv	Oraenv command for Cshell	(7.3.4)
csscan	Character Set Scanner	8.1.7
ctxkbtc	InterMedia	8.1.5
ctxload	InterMedia	(7.3.4)
ctxsrv	InterMedia	(7.3.4)
cursize	Cursor Size Tool	8.0
dbca	Database Creation Assistant	9.0.1
dbfmig	Datafile Migrator	8.1.5
dbfsize	Datafile Size	(7.3.4)
dbhome	displays Oracle$HOME	(7.3.4)
dbshut	shuts down Oracle	(7.3.4)
dbsnmp	Intelligent Agent	8.0
dbsnmpj	Intelligent Agent Job Processor (not Java or JRE)	9.0.1
dbsnmpwd	Intelligent Agent	9.0.1
dbstart	Starts Oracle	(7.3.4)
dbua	Database Upgrade Assistant	9.2.0
dbv	Verifies datafiles	(7.3.4)
debugproxy	Oracle JVM Debugging	8.1.7
demobld	Table Build for Oracle Developer demo	(7.3.4)
demodrop	Table drop for Oracle Developer demo	(7.3.4)
deploync	JAR file deployment	8.1.7
dgmgrl	Data Manager	9.0.1
dropjava	Drops java objects	8.1.5
dumpsga	Dumps SGA contents	9.2.0
echodo	Echo command and print it	(7.3.4)
ela	Enterprise Login Assistant	9.0.1

Binary	Description	First Available
emca	(Enterprise Manager?)	9.0.1
emwebsite	(Enterprise Manager?)	9.0.1
Esm	Enterprise Security Manager Command Line Utility	9.2.0
exp	Export	(7.3.4)
extproc	External Process Agent	8.0
extractlib	Extract objects from a list of libraries	(7.3.4)
fmputl	File mapping	9.2.0
fmputlhp	File mapping	9.2.0
genagtsh	Agent shared library generation	8.1.5
genclntsh	Generate shared client library for OCI, Pro*C and XA	(7.3.4)
genksms	Generate ksms.s to relocate SGA	8.0
gennfgt	Generate list of native network libraries - nnfgt.o	8.0
gennttab	Generate list of SQL*Net protocol adapters -Output written to ntcontab.s	8.0
genoccish	Generate OCCI shared object	9.2.0
gensyslib	Generate list of operating system libraries to be linked into executables. Output written to $ORACLE_HOME/lib/sysliblist	(7.3.4)
helpins	Install SQL*Plus help system	(7.3.4)
hsalloci	Heterogeneous Agent	8.1.5
hsdepxa	Heterogeneous Agent	8.1.5
hsodbc	Heterogeneous Services ODBC	8.1.6
hsots	Heterogeneous Services Oracle Transaction Service	8.1.5
imp	Import	(7.3.4)
isqlplus	Browser based SQL*Plus interface	9.2.0
jpub	Publish Java classes	8.1.5
kgmgr	Net Configuration Assistant	8.1.6
kgpmon	Unknown	8.1.5
ldapadd	LDAP management	8.1.6
ldapaddmt	LDAP management	8.1.6
ldapbind	LDAP management	8.1.6
ldapcompare	LDAP management	8.1.6
ldapdelete	LDAP management	8.1.6
ldapmoddn	LDAP management	8.1.6
ldapmodify	LDAP management	8.1.6
ldapmodifymt	LDAP management	8.1.6

Binary	Description	First Available
ldapsearch	LDAP management	8.1.6
ldifmigrator	OID Migration Tool	9.2.0
ldifwrite	Oracle Internet Directory - write LDIF file	8.1.6
lmsgen	Binary message file generation	8.1.5
loadjava	loads java objects	8.1.5
loadpsp	loads pl/sql server pages	8.1.6
lsnrctl	Listener control	(7.3.4)
lxchknlb	Net Configuration Assistant	(7.3.4)
lxegen	NLS Calendar	(7.3.4)
lxinst	NLS Data Install	(7.3.4)
mapsga	Provides SGA map	9.2.0
maxmem	Displays RAM stats	(7.3.4)
mig	Migrate	(7.3.4)
migprep	Migrate Prepare	8.1.5
modada		9.2.0
names	Oracle Names	8.1.6
namesctl	Oracle Names Control	8.1.6
ncomp	Native Compiler (Java)	8.1.7
netca	Net Configuration Assistant	8.1.5
netmgr	Net Assistant	9.0.1
Nid	Set new database ID	9.2.0
Nmu7q28	Oracle Intelligent Agent	9.0.1
nmudg	Oracle Intelligent Agent	9.0.1
nmumigr8	Oracle Data Gatherer	9.0.1
ociconv	Convert OCI source from short (8.0.1) to long (8.0.2) function names	8.0
ocm	Oracle Change Manager	9.0.1
odisrv	Oracle Internet Directory	9.0.1
odisrvreg	Oracle Internet Directory	9.0.1
oemLaunchOms	Oracle Mgmt. Server	9.0.1
oemapp	Oracle Enterprise Manager	8.1.6
oemctl	OEM Control	9.0.1
Oemevent	Oracle Intelligent Agent	8.1.5
oerr	Error Lookup	(7.3.4)
oidadmin	Oracle Internet Directory	8.1.6
oidctl	Oracle Internet Directory	8.1.7
oidldapd	Oracle Internet Directory	9.2.0
oidmon	Oracle Internet Directory	8.1.7
oidpasswd	Oracle Internet Directory	8.1.6
oidprovtool	Oracle Internet Directory	9.2.0
oidreconcile	Oracle Internet Directory	8.1.7
oidrepld	Oracle Internet Directory	9.2.0
ojspc	JSP Compiler	9.0.1
okdstry	Delete Kerberos ticket	8.1.7
okinit	New Kerberos ticket	8.1.7

Binary	Description	First Available
oklist	Check Kerberos ticket	8.1.6
onrsd	Oracle Names	8.0
oracg	Class Generator	9.0.1
oracle	Oracle executable	(7.3.4)
oradism	Dynamic ISM	9.0.1
oraenv	Manages environment	(7.3.4)
orapwd	Manages passwords	(7.3.4)
oratclsh	TCL Shell	8.0
oraxml	XML Processor	9.0.1
oraxsl	XSLT Processor	9.0.1
osh	Called from oraenv	8.0
otrccol	Oracle trace collector	(7.3.4)
otrccref	Oracle trace purge collect.dat file	(7.3.4)
otrcfmt	Oracle trace format	(7.3.4)
otrcrep	Oracle trace report	(7.3.4)
ott	Object Type Translator	8.0
ott8	Object Type Translator	9.0.1
owm	Oracle Wallet Manager	8.1.6
passwdconvert	Unknown	9.2.0
proc	Pro*C	(7.3.4)
procob	Pro*COBOL	(7.3.4)
procob18	Pro*COBOL	8.1.6
Profor	Pro*Fortran	8.1.6
relink	Relink exeutables	8.1.5
rman	Recovery Manager	8.0
rtsora	COBOL Runtime System	(7.3.4)
runInstaller	Net Configuration Assistant	8.1.5
sbttest	Media Manager	8.1.5
schema	XML validation	9.0.1
schemasync	synchronizes schema elements; used with Oracle Directory Server	9.2.0
sqlj	SQLJ	8.1.5
sqlldr	SQL*Loader	(7.3.4)
sqlplus	SQL*Plus	(7.3.4)
statusnc	Native Compilation Status	8.1.7
symfind	Symbolic find	(7.3.4)
sysresv	Shared Memory / Semaphores	8.1.5
tkprof	Trace output formatter	(7.3.4)
tns2nis	TNS NIS Mapping	8.1.6
tnslsnr	TNS Listener	(7.3.4)
tnsping	Listener pinger	(7.3.4)
transx	XML	9.2.0
trcasst	Trace Assistant	8.0
trcroute	Network analysis	(7.3.4)

Binary	Description	First Available
tstshm	Shared memory	(7.3.4)
umu	LDAP	9.2.0
unzip	Unzip utility	9.2.0
wrap	PL/SQL encrypter	(7.3.4)
xml	XML / XSL processing	9.0.1
xmlcg	XML processing	9.2.0
xsql	XSQL Pages	9.0.1
zip	Zip Utility	9.2.0

Table 2.2 – UNIX *Binaries Provided in Oracel 9.2.*

Windows Executables

The table below lists the Windows executables provided by Oracle. Many of the utilities provided in UNIX are also available in Windows. The list below has been restricted to those utilities that are only present on the Windows platform.

Executable	Description	First Available
dbsnmp.exe	Intelligent Agent	8.1.5
dbsnmpj.exe	Intelligent Agent Job Processor (nothing to do with Java or JRE)	8.1.5
encaps.exe	SNMP encapsulation agent	Default in 9.0.1 Custom in 8i and below
encsvc.exe	SNMP encapsulation service	Default in 9.0.1 Custom in 8i and below
launch.exe	Java code launcher	8.0
launchem.exe	Enterprise Manager Launcher	8.0
ocopy.exe	File copy utility	(7.3.4)
OMSNTsrv.exe	Oracle Management Server	9.2.0
omtsreco.exe	MTS Recovery	9.0.1
OO4OCODEWIZ.EXE	Oracle Objects for OLE Code Wizard	9.2.0

Executable	Description	First Available
OracleAdNetConnect.exe	MFC Application	8.1.7
OracleAdNetTest.exe	MFC Application	9.0.1
oradim.exe	Manages oracle instances	(7.3.4)
orakill.exe	Process killer	(7.3.4)
oramts_deinst.exe	Unknown	9.2.0
Orastack.exe	Modifies stack RAM	(7.3.4)
Pagntsrv.exe	OEM Paging Server	9.0.1
tdvapp.exe	Trace Data Viewer	9.0.1
VDOShell.exe	Oracle Expert	9.0.1
vmq.exe	SQL Analyze	9.0.1
Vtushell.exe	OEM Index Tuning Wizard	9.0.1
xpautune.exe	Oracle Expert	9.0.1
xpcoin.exe	Oracle Expert	9.0.1
xpksh.exe	Oracle Expert Command Shell	9.0.1
xpui.exe	Oracle Expert	9.0.1

Table 2.3 - Utilities that are only present on the Windows platform.

Summary

This chapter defined a utility in terms relevant to an Oracle professional. The DBA now has a list of available utilities, as well as a mechanism to discover them in the future – be it binary executables, supplied Oracle packages, new instance parameters, system events, or new *v$* views.

This chapter listed many potential Oracle utilities, those that reside in either the database itself or the *$ORACLE_HOME/bin* directory. The next chapter will begin the exploration and detailed analysis of the most useful Oracle utilities. The journey will begin by discussing those utilities that the DBA can use for general administration functions.

Chapter 3

Utilities for General Administration

The Oracle supplied utilities have been loosely categorized throughout the course of this book. Some utilities are difficult to categorize, especially the more obscure and generic ones.

This chapter examines the utilities that a DBA can use to manage the Oracle environment. Utilities that pertain to killing threads, obtaining error messages, and altering session stack size will all be discussed in this chapter.

Terminating Threads with *orakill*

The *orakill* utility is provided only with Oracle databases on Windows platforms. The executable (*orakill.exe*) is available to DBAs to kill Oracle sessions directly from the DOS command line without requiring any connection to the database.

In the UNIX world, a DBA can kill a shadow process by issuing the *kill –9* command from the UNIX prompt. UNIX is able to provide this capability given that the UNIX operating system is based on processes that fork other processes. All processes can be listed by using the *ps* UNIX command. The Oracle background processes will be listed separately from all of the Oracle sessions since they have their own process.

Unlike the UNIX operating system, Windows systems are thread-based. For each instance, the background processes and sessions are all contained within the *oracle.exe* executable. These processes are not listed in the "Processes" tab of Windows Task Manager. Each session creates its own thread within *oracle.exe* and therefore, is not exposed to the Windows user. Killing the *oracle.exe* process in Windows would crash the entire database.

The *orakill* utility serves the same purpose as *kill – 9* in UNIX . The command requires the instance and the SPID of the thread to kill. The utility will display exactly how to obtain the SPID in the event the command was entered without parameters:

```
C:\oracle9i\bin>orakill

Usage:  orakill sid thread

  where sid    = the Oracle instance to target
        thread = the thread id of the thread to kill

  The thread id should be retrieved from the spid column of a query
such as:

        select spid, osuser, s.program from
        v$process p, v$session s where p.addr=s.paddr
```

If the statement suggested by Oracle (above) to retrieve the Thread ID is executed, the results below are displayed:

```
select a.username, a.osuser, b.spid
   from v$session a, v$process b
   where a.paddr = b.addr
     and a.username is not null;
```

```
USERNAME                       OSUSER                         SPID
------------------------------ ------------------------------ -----
SCOTT                          Scott                          3116
AMOORE                         Alex                           4760
DMOORE                         Dave                            768
```

With the SPID for each user listed above, the session for any user can be killed.

```
C:\oracle9i\bin>orakill ORCL92 4760

Kill of thread id 4760 in instance ORCL92 successfully signalled.


SQL> select a.username, a.osuser, b.spid
  2  from v$session a, v$process b
  3  where a.paddr = b.addr
  4  and a.username is not null;


USERNAME                       OSUSER                         SPID
------------------------------ ------------------------------ -----
SCOTT                          Scott                          3116
DMOORE                         Dave                            768

2 rows selected.
```

Notice that SPID 4760, user AMOORE is gone.

Why does Oracle provide a utility to kill sessions from the DOS prompt, when a DBA could kill a user session from within Oracle? The following command will also kill the user session:

```
alter system kill session(sid, serial#);
```

The *sid* (session ID) and *serial#* above can be obtained from the *v$session* view. There are a couple of reasons a DBA might use *orakill* instead of the *alter system kill session* command.

1. **The *alter system* statement will not clear any locks that exist.** Instead, the session

will remain connected until it times out, then the session is killed and the locks are released. The *orakill* command will kill the thread and the locks instantly.

2. **A DBA may be unable to gain access to a SQL prompt due to a runaway query consuming all database resources.** In this case, the session can be killed without ever logging in to the database.

These are good reasons to kill threads directly from the DOS prompt, but they do not address how to get the required kill information from the database if access is unavailable. How can a DBA obtain the SPID?

One way to obtain the Oracle SPID is to use a tool like QuickSlice from Microsoft (free download) that will display Windows threads and their IDs. The QuickSlice main screen (Figure 3.1) displays each executable that is active in the operating system.

The entries listed in QuickSlice match those displayed in the Windows Task Manager. QuickSlice also displays the amount of the CPU being used by an executable, as does the Task Manager.

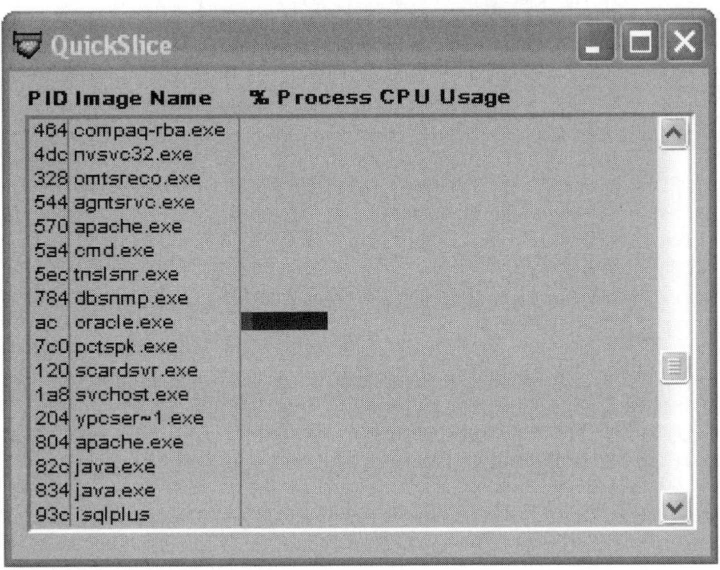

Figure 3.1 – QuickSlice Main Screen

The DBA can use the main QuickSlice screen to determine the CPU-intensive executables, and drill down into the threads for more information.

The next QuickSlice window (Figure 3.2) displays the threads for a given executable (*oracle.exe*). In the example below, TID 300 is using the CPU.

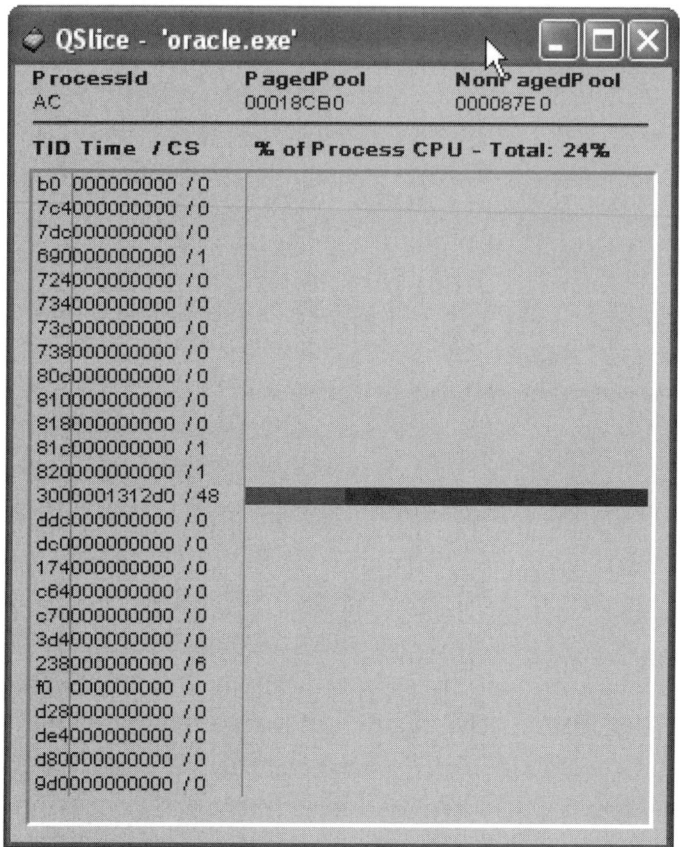

Figure 3.2 – QuickSlice Thread Window

The DBA can quickly identify the most consumptive thread and decide what to do. The TID column (Thread ID) in QuickSlice is a Hex value and matches the decimal value for the *spid* column from *v$session.* In this case, the TID consuming the CPU is 300 (Hex), which equals Session spid 768 (Decimal). Therefore, the command to kill this session would be:

```
C:\oracle9i\bin>orakill ORCL92 768
```

In this example, the thread (Oracle session) was killed in the operating system without ever logging into the database. Before killing the session, the DBA may decide to view the SQL being executed by the session. This can be obtained by using the TID above (300) in the following SQL statement:

```
select b.username, a.sql_text from
v$sqltext_with_newlines a, v$session b, v$process c
where    c.spid  = to_number('300', 'xxx')
    and  c.addr  = b.paddr
    and  b.sql_address = a.address;
```

Tips for using *orakill*

- **The *orakill* utility should be used as a last resort only.** If the session cannot be killed more gracefully (via *alter system kill session*), or the instance is inaccessible via SQL, then *orakill* should be used to terminate the offending session.

- **Background processes should not be terminated, mainly user sessions.** Killing a background process like SMON or PMON can cause serious Oracle errors and can bring the database down. To confirm that it is not a background session being killed, the following query can be used to identify the SPID for each background process:

```
select c.name, b.spid, a.sid
from v$session a, v$process b, v$bgprocess c
where c.paddr  <> '00'
   and c.paddr =  b.addr
   and b.addr  =  a.paddr;
```

```
NAME  SPID                SID
----- ------------ ----------
PMON  1680                  1
DBW0  1828                  2
LGWR  1844                  3
CKPT  1852                  4
SMON  1848                  5
RECO  2060                  6
CJQ0  2064                  7
QMN0  2072                  8
```

- **Access to the Windows machine containing the database must be secure.** Any user with access to the box could access *orakill* or the Windows Task Manager and damage database processes.

- The DBA may decide to use operating system utilities to kill sessions and monitor Oracle CPU utilization. Starting at the operating system level is an effective technique employed by many seasoned DBAs.

Viewing Errors with the *oerr* Utility

The *oerr* utility (Oracle Error) is provided only with Oracle databases on UNIX platforms. *oerr* is not an executable, but instead, a shell script that retrieves messages from installed message files. The utility is not provided on Windows systems, since it uses *awk* commands to retrieve the requested text from the file. However, later in this chapter, a Windows-based implementation will be provided.

The syntax required of the *oerr* utility is:

```
oerr <facility> <error>
```

The facility is the prefix to the error number. These include ORA, PLS, EXP, etc. The error is the actual error number returned by Oracle.

For example, if the database returned an ORA-12544 error, the following *oerr* command would be executed to gain more information:

```
$ oerr ora 12544

12544, 00000, "TNS:contexts have different wait/test functions"
// *Cause: Two protocol adapters have conflicting wait/test functions.
// *Action:  Not normally visible to the user. For further details, turn
// on tracing and reexecute the operation. If error persists, contact
// Oracle Customer Support.
```

Notice that Oracle returned the "Cause" of the error and recommended "Action". This is usually the case, however many error codes exist with no cause or action text available.

How *oerr* Works

To best understand exactly how *oerr* works, review the shell script. The *oerr.ksh* script is provided by Oracle in the *$ORACLE_HOME/bin* directory.

The commands in the *oerr.ksh* shell script confirm that *$ORACLE_HOME* is set, and if not, the program terminates. Next, the facility information is read from the facility file located in $*ORACLE_HOME/lib/facility.lis.* Below is a portion of the *facility.lis* file. The facility file contains three mandatory data items and one optional. The mandatory data items include the facility, component, and the name of the alias for the component, if one exists, otherwise a "*" will be used. In the file below, "ora" is the facility, "rdbms" is the component, and it does not have an alias "*". The optional data item is the description, which none are provided in the file below.

Facility.lis file

```
o2u:precomp:*:
oae:oacore:*:
oao:office:*:
obk:obackup:ebu:
oci:rdbms:*:
ofc:office:*:
oma:office:*:
omapi:office:*:
omb:office:*:
omd:office:*:
omgut:office:*:
omkt:office:*:
omu:office:*:
omv:office:*:
opw:rdbms:*:
ora:rdbms:*:
osn:network:*:
osnq:network:*:
pcb:precomp:*:
pcbe:precomp:*:
pcc:precomp:*:
pcf:precomp:*:
pcg:precomp:*:
pci:precomp:*:
pcm:plsql:*:
pcp:precomp:*:
pcs:precomp:*:
pg2:precomp:*:
pgo:precomp:*:
pgp:precomp:*:
pls:plsql:*:
```

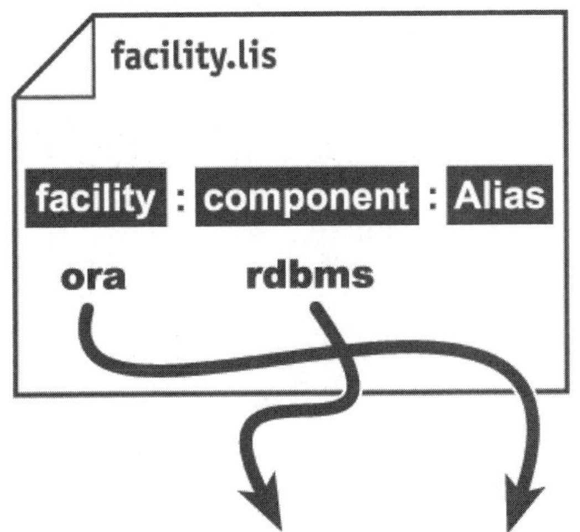

Figure 3.3 – oerr Architecture

Using the facility name that was entered on the command line, *oerr* retrieves the component for that facility (as displayed in Figure 3.3). In the example above (*oerr* ora 04030), *oerr* will use the *rdbms* component. Once the component is retrieved, *oerr* can derive the full path and file name for the appropriate message file:

```
Msg_File=$ORACLE_HOME/$Component/mesg/${Facility}us.msg
```

Following the example through, the line above equates to the following directory and file:

```
$ORACLE_HOME/rdbms/mesg/oraus.msg
```

Once the path and filename are determined, the contents of the file will provide the cause and action for each error in the facility:

```
01058, 00000, "internal New Upi interface error"
// *Cause: Attempt to delete non existant hstdef extension.
// *Action: Report as a bug.
01059, 00000, "parse expected before a bind or execute"
// *Cause: The client application attempted to bind a variable or execute
//         a cursor opened in a PL/SQL block before the statement was parsed.
// *Action: Ensure the statement is parsed before a bind or execute.
01060, 00000, "array binds or executes not allowed"
// *Cause: The client application attempted to bind an array of cursors or
//         attempted to repeatedly execute against a PL/SQL block with a bind
//         variable of type cursor.
// *Action: Bind a single cursor or execute the PL/SQL block once.
```

All of the "ORA" error messages are contained in this file. *oerr* will find the error number in this file utilizing *awk* commands and display the results back to the terminal.

oerr on Windows

oerr is only available on UNIX , but it does not take much code to access the same message file and display the same messages on a Windows machine. To do this, the actual message file must be *ftp'd* from a UNIX host to the Windows machine and placed in the same directory as the Java program.

The Java program below (*oerr.java*) reads the message file and displays the text associated with the error code:

oerr.java

```
/**
 * Title:        oerr
 * Description:  Oracle oerr utility for Windows
 * @author Dave Moore
 * @version 1.0
 */

import java.io.*;

public class oerr {

static final String badCommand = "Usage: oerr facility error \n" +
 "Facility is identified by the prefix string in the error message.\n" +
 "For example, if you get ORA-04030, \"ora\" is the facility and \"04030\"\n" +
 "is the error.  So you should type \"oerr ora 04030\". \n" +
 "\n" +
 "If you get LCD-111, type \"oerr lcd 111\", and so on.\n";

  public static void main (String args[]) {

     if (args.length < 1) {
        System.out.println(badCommand);
        System.exit(0);
      }

     String fileName    = null;

     if (args[0].equalsIgnoreCase("ora"))
         fileName = "oraus.msg";
     else {
         System.out.println("No message file available for that facility");
         System.exit(0);
     }

     try {

        FileReader fr = new FileReader( fileName );
        BufferedReader br = new BufferedReader(fr);
        String lineOfText;
        while (!(null==(lineOfText=br.readLine()))) {
           if (!lineOfText.startsWith("//"))  {
              if (lineOfText.startsWith(args[1])) {
                 System.out.println(lineOfText);
                 while ((lineOfText=br.readLine()).startsWith("/")) {
                    System.out.println(lineOfText);
                 }
             }
           }
        } // while

        br.close();
        fr.close();
     }
     catch (Exception e) {
        System.out.println("Exception occurred: " + e);
     }
}
}
```

This program was designed to resemble *oerr* on UNIX as much as possible. It processes facility names, though the ORA facility is the only one used in this program. Other facilities and their message files could easily be added to the program.

The Java program reads the message file line by line until it encounters the actual error code. While it does take more time to retrieve an error message located at the end of the file, the message is returned within a second, even when processing large message files.

To execute this program would require the following syntax:

```
C:\oracle9i\bin\java oerr ora 00942
```

To make it easier to execute the program and make it resemble *oerr* even more, the *oerr.bat* file below can be created to insulate the user from typing the "java" keyword on the command line.

oerr.bat

```
@echo off
java oerr %1 %2
```

Executing the bat file above from the DOS prompt, the command will work exactly as it does in UNIX:

```
C:\oracle9i\bin\oerr ora 00942
00942, 00000, "table or view does not exist"
// *Cause:
// *Action:
```

The next section will specify a way to deal with the apparent lack of information in the output listed above.

Creating Custom Message Files

The good thing about *oerr* is that it is always there to use. Similar to the *VI* text editor in UNIX , *oerr* will be on every Oracle UNIX server. The challenge is to augment the supplied Oracle messages with your own, tailored to your specific environment.

Rather than editing the message files provided by Oracle, it is better to create new ones. This way, the message files are insulated from Oracle releases and the contents retained, without losing any new Oracle text. For instance, if the text in the Oracle supplied file was modified, what would happen when the next release of Oracle provides more text on the same error? That new information would be lost, and the changes would need to be made again in the new supplied message files.

A much better option is to create a customized facility and component. That way, any Oracle expertise is retained in the Oracle supplied message files, while customized, specific information is added to the new message files. Then, instead of executing *oerr* and receiving these weak results:

```
$ oerr ora 00942
00942, 00000, "table or view does not exist"
// *Cause:
// *Action:
```

The following *oerr* command could be used to provide output from the customized message file:

```
$ oerr mycompany 00942

00942, 00000, "table or view does not exist"
// *Cause: A lot of things can cause this error, however, the
//         most frequent one in our shop is trying to access
//         a table or view in another users schema.  You do
//         not have access to that schema and therefore Oracle
//         says it doesn't exist for you to see.
// *Action: Try fully qualifying the table or view name
//         (scott.table1).  Verify that you have privileges to the
//         object you're trying to access.
```

Notice the only difference is the new facility "mycompany", which points to its own message file. A customized message file can be created in three easy steps:

1. Add the facility to the *facility.lis* file.
2. Create a directory that contains the new message file.
3. Create the actual message file.

oerr Alternatives

The greatest weakness of the *oerr* utility is the content of its messages. Getting rapid feedback about a particular error seems desirable until text like the following is returned:

```
$ oerr ora 00942
00942, 00000, "table or view does not exist"
// *Cause:
// *Action:
```

Getting paged at 2:00 AM is not fun, especially when *oerr* does not provide a "cause" and "action" for the error. Fortunately, there are two alternatives to *oerr* that do a better job of analyzing and resolving the problem.

- **Oracle TechNet** – The TechNet site (http://technet.oracle.com) can be a lifesaver. Full documentation is available online, including error messages. TechNet is available to anyone that registers online.

- **Oracle Metalink** – This is the online support database (http://metalink.oracle.com) for Oracle. Operated by Oracle Corporation Support Services personnel, this site is likely to have the solution for a problem. A "quick search" capability specifies problem solutions.

The *oerr* utility should be used for quick identification of problem descriptions and actions. Custom facilities and message files can be created to respond to frequent errors specific to your environment. For detailed problem descriptions and analysis, access either TechNet or Metalink over the Internet.

Memory Utilities

Utilities exist for both Windows and UNIX systems that help DBAs deal with memory issues. The *orastack* utility exists on Windows systems, while the *maxmem* utility can be helpful in UNIX. The *orastack* utility is only available to Oracle databases on Windows platforms. It is used primarily to address the ORA-04030 error on Windows servers. The *oerr* output for the ORA-04030 error is:

```
04030, 00000, "out of process memory when trying to allocate %s
bytes (%s,%s)"
// *Cause:  Operating system process private memory has been
exhausted
// *Action:
```

This error occurs when Oracle is trying to allocate memory for the session but none exists. Windows NT has a limitation of 2 GB of RAM allocated for user processes and a maximum of 2 GB for the system. The memory counter reaches the maximum addressable memory at 2 GB, and the ORA-04030 error will occur.

To conserve memory, the amount allocated for each connection process could be reduced as it is established, using the *sort area size* parameter of the instances. The *orastack* utility can accomplish this. Since it functions strictly at the operating system level, there is nothing that can be done inside Oracle to limit the memory obtained upon a user connection.

The syntax of the command is the *orastack* keyword followed by the executable file name:

```
C:\oracle9i\bin\orastack oracle.exe

Current Reserved Memory per Thread  = 1048576
Current Committed Memory Per Thread = 4096
```

When the command is executed without specifying a new size (as above), the utility simply displays the memory usage and does not change anything.

The reserved memory is that which is allocated and not backed up by a data store. The committed memory is that which is allocated and supported by a data store of some sort (pagefile, physical memory pages).

Notice the "Reserved Memory per Thread" of 1MB above. Each connection to the database will instantly grab a megabyte of RAM. The Oracle executable cannot be active when the command to reduce the size of the stack is executed. Once the executable is inactive, the *orastack* utility can be used to safely reduce the memory acquired on connection.

```
C:\oracle9i\bin\orastack oracle.exe 500000
```

After the command is executed, each session that connects to the database will consume 500K of RAM on connection. 500K should be the absolute lowest value to set this parameter.

The resetting of this value for *oracle.exe* applies only to local (non-SQL*Net) connections. For connections that are initiated from the listener, the stacks on the *tnslsnr.exe* executable can be reduced by running *orastack* against *tnslsnr.exe*. This is where most connections to the database will originate.

```
C:\oracle9i\bin\orastack tnslsnr.exe 500000
```

The *orastack* utility can be used on any executable that initiates database connections.

Even though *orastack* is only available for Windows systems, other memory utilities exist on the UNIX platform. The *maxmem* utility can be used on UNIX systems to determine when the ORA-04300 error will occur. Utilizing this utility, the DBA can calculate the number of sessions that can connect to the database before the ORA-04030 error message is encountered.

The *maxmem* utility is a simple program with no command-line options:

```
$ maxmem
Memory starts at:      141728 (    229a0)
Memory ends at:     268025856 ( ff9c000)
Memory available:   267884128 ( ff79660)
```

The *maxmem* utility returns three data items, although only one is really useful to the DBA. "Memory available" indicates the number of bytes of RAM that are available. This is critical to know since ORA-04030 errors will occur when this number is less than 1,000,000 (1 MB).

If another session connects to the database, the *maxmem* utility will reflect a reduction in the memory available:

```
SQL> connect scott/tiger@ASG920;

Connected.

$ maxmem

Memory starts at:      141728 (    229a0)
Memory ends at:     267075583 ( feb3fff)
Memory available:   266933855 ( fe9165f)
```

Based on the delta in the memory available, the memory consumed by this one connection to the database is 950273 bytes, roughly 1 MB. Subsequent tests indicate that memory allocated for each connection may vary, but it is always close to 1 MB. Given that a session on this host will grab 1 MB of RAM, *awk* can be used as part of the *maxmem* command to indicate the number of sessions it will be able to support.

```
$ maxmem | awk  '$2 ~ /available/ {printf("%s%d\n","# Future
Sessions: ",$3/1024/1024)}'

# Future Sessions: 251
```

This command will display the third field (divided by 1 MB) of any output line that contains "available" in the second field. This number will represent the number of additional sessions that can be handled by the database, assuming that each will take 1 MB. Based on the above output, the database can handle approximately 251 database connections before an Oracle memory error occurs. This number is an approximation based on the earlier benchmark that measured 1 MB for the connection. The DBA should include this command as part of their regular Oracle monitoring scripts on UNIX databases.

Utilities for Starting and Stopping Databases

Oracle provides two UNIX scripts that assist DBAs with starting and stopping the database: *dbstart* and *dbshut*. For Windows platforms, the

oradim utility is provided for starting and stopping the Oracle instance.
The *dbstart* utility reads the *oratab* file, shown in the example below. The oratab file will reside in either */etc* or */var/opt/oracle*, depending on the UNIX version. It contains three data items separated by colons:

```
ASG920xr:/usr/oracle/9.2.0:Y
ASG817xr:/usr/oracle/8.1.7:Y
TEST920xr:/usr/oracle/9.2.0:N
PROD920xr:/usr/oracle/9.2.0:N
```

The first field is the Oracle SID. The second field is the home directory for that Oracle SID. The Y or N instructs Oracle whether to start or stop the particular database when either the *dbstart* or *dbshut* command is issued. The *dbstart* command simply parses the *oratab* file and starts those databases that have a Y in the third field. It also uses the *ORACLE_HOME* specified in the file to connect internally to the database and issue the *startup* command.

The *dbstart* command can be added to the UNIX servers' initialization or run level scripts. This enables *dbstart* to be executed each time the machine is booted or when it changes run levels. The method for implementing this is platform specific, as we see below.

Auto Start on HP-UX and Solaris

For HP-UX version 10 and above, the system initialization scripts are contained in */etc/rc<n>.d* directories, where "n" is the operating system run-level. These directories contain scripts that begin with a K or S, followed by a number, and then a file name (S75cron). All scripts that begin with "S" are executed at system startup in ascending order of their number. Scripts beginning with "K" (*Kill*) are called at system shutdown time.

As a general rule of thumb, the Oracle startup script should have a high sequence number (S99dbstart), which will ensure that other system processes have been started prior to Oracle. Likewise, the *kill* scripts should have a low sequence number in order to shutdown Oracle early in the process (K01dbshut).

Auto Start on AIX

For AIX servers, the system initialization file is */etc/inittab* and the initialization script is */etc/rc*. A utility (*/usr/sbin/mkitab*) can be used to make an entry in the inittab file. The shutdown script for AIX is */usr/sbin/shutdown*, although it should not be modified to support *dbshut*.

To add the *dbstart* utility to the AIX initialization process, the following steps can be performed:

1. **Create the script /etc/rc.oracle.** The script should contain the following:

```
su oracle <<EOF
<$ORACLE_HOME>/bin/dbstart
EOF
```

2. **Add the script to the inittab using the *mkitab* utility.**

```
$ /usr/sbin/mkitab "rcoracle:2:wait:/etc.rc.oracle
>/dev/console 2>&1"
```

All references to *<$ORACLE_HOME>* should be replaced with the actual Oracle Home directory. Now upon system startup, the *dbstart* utility is invoked at run level 2.

Starting and Stopping on Windows

The *dbstart* and *dbstop* shell scripts do not exist on Windows platforms. Consequently Oracle database startup and shutdown is implemented completely differently. The *oradim* utility is used on the Windows platform to perform these tasks.

```
C:\oracle9i\bin\oradim -startup -sid ORCL92 -usrpwd manager
-starttype SRVC,INST -pfile C:\oracle9i\admin\ORCL92\pfile\init.ora
```

- ***startup*** – Indicates that the specified instance should be started.
- ***sid*** – The SID of the database to start.
- ***usrpwd*** – The password for the database user.
- ***starttype*** – Specifies whether to start the instance, the service, or both (SRVC, INST).

The following command can be used to shutdown the instance with *oradim*:

```
C:\oracle9i\bin\oradim -shutdown -sid ORCL92 -shuttype SRVC,INST
-shutmode A
```

Notice that no password is needed to perform this task.

The *shuttype* parameter specifies what is to be stopped – the service (SRVC), the instance (INST), or both (SRVC, INST). The *shutmode* specifies the method that should perform the shutdown – (A)bort, (I)mmediate, or (N)ormal.

Each operation, regardless of success, is logged in the *oradim* log file (*ORACLE_HOME\database\OraDim.Log*). This file should be checked for errors after each *oradim* command is executed.

The *oradim* utility provides more than just the ability to start and stop Windows databases. *oradim* can create and edit databases. It also allows DBAs to configure script-based installation mechanisms, bypassing the Oracle Database Configuration Assistant's graphical user interface (GUI).

For a reference of all *oradim* commands, use the *oradim –help* command.

oraenv and *coraenv* Utilities

The *oraenv* and *coraenv* utilities both aid in setting the Oracle environment on UNIX systems (other utilities exist on Windows platform that enable the Oracle Home to be set.) The *coraenv* utility is appropriate for the UNIX C Shell; *oraenv* should be used with either the Bourne or Korn shells.

Database operations require the *ORACLE_HOME* to be set before the user may access the database. If *ORACLE_HOME* is not set, commands such as *sqlplus, exp,* or any other utility for that matter, will not be found.

Both utilities are shell scripts that do the same thing in the different UNIX shells. They will prompt for a *SID* of the database unless *ORAENV_ASK* is set to N. The utility will also append the *ORACLE_HOME* value to the path, marking the location of the utility.

The *oraenv* command will prompt for the *SID* of the database that you wish *$ORACLE_HOME* to access.

```
$ . oraenv
ORACLE_SID = [] ? ASG920
```

The *dbhome* utility can now be used to verify that *$ORACLE_HOME* is correct.

```
$ dbhome
/usr/oracle/9.2.0
```

The "dot space" part of the command is required to make the environment change with the parent shell, as opposed to entering a command without it which would only affect the subshell running that process.

These commands can be used to avoid specifying the network service name when issuing commands.

For instance, without using *oraenv*, an *sqlplus* command would look like:

```
$ sqlplus system/manager@nameofservice as sysdba
```

whereas after *oraenv* has been executed, the following command would work:

```
$ sqlplus system/manager as sysdba
```

Using *orapwd* to Connect Remotely as SYSDBA

The Oracle *orapwd* utility assists the DBA with granting SYSDBA and SYSOPER privileges to other users. By default, the user SYS is the only user that has these privileges. Creating a password file via *orapwd* enables remote users to connect with administrative privileges through SQL*Net.

The SYSOPER privilege allows instance startup, shutdown, mount, and dismount. It allows the DBA to perform general database maintenance without viewing user data. The SYSDBA privilege is the same as *connect internal* was in prior versions. It provides the ability to do everything, unrestricted.

If *orapwd* has not yet been executed, attempting to grant SYSDBA or SYSOPER privileges will result in the following error:

```
SQL> grant sysdba to scott;
ORA-01994: GRANT failed: cannot add users to public password file
```

The following steps can be performed to grant other users these privileges:

1. **Create the password file**. This is done by executing the following command:

   ```
   $ orapwd file=filename  password=password entries=max_users
   ```

   The *filename* is the name of the file that will hold the password information. The file location will default to the current directory unless the full path is specified. The contents are encrypted and are unreadable. The *password* required is the one for the SYS user of the database.

   The *max_users* is the number of database users that can be granted SYSDBA or SYSOPER. This parameter should be set to a higher value than the number of anticipated users to prevent having to delete and recreate the password file.

2. **Edit the *init.ora* parameter *remote_login_passwordfile***. This parameter must be set to either SHARED or EXCLUSIVE. When set to SHARED, the password file can be used by multiple databases, yet only the SYS user is recognized. When set to EXCLUSIVE, the file can be used by only one database, yet multiple users can exist in the file. The parameter setting can be confirmed by:

```
SQL> show parameter password

NAME                                 TYPE        VALUE
------------------------------------ ----------- ----------
remote_login_passwordfile            string      EXCLUSIVE
```

3. **Grant SYSDBA or SYSOPER to users.** When SYSDBA or SYSOPER privileges are granted to a user, that user's name and privilege information are added to the password file.

```
SQL> grant sysdba to scott;

Grant succeeded.
```

4. **Confirm that the user is listed in the password file.**

```
SQL> select * from v$pwfile_users;

USERNAME                       SYSDBA SYSOPER
------------------------------ ------ -------
SYS                            TRUE   TRUE
SCOTT                          TRUE   FALSE
```

Now the user SCOTT can connect as SYSDBA. Administrative users can be connected and authenticated to a local or remote database by using the SQL*Plus *connect* command. They must connect using their username and password, and with the AS SYSDBA or AS SYSOPER clause:

```
SQL> connect scott/tiger as sysdba;
Connected.
```

The DBA utilizes the *orapwd* utility to grant SYSDBA and SYSOPER privileges to other database users. The SYS password should never be shared and should be highly classified.

Summary

This chapter covered general database administration utilities that can benefit the DBA. The *orakill* utility can be used on Windows to kill database connection threads based on their process ID. Multiple ways of addressing the ORA-04030 error were also outlined. On Windows systems, the *orastack* utility can be used to reduce the initial memory consumption of the connection. For UNIX , the *maxmem* utility can be used to predict when the ORA-04030 error will occur. When errors do occur in Oracle, the *oerr* utility provides more information. The chapter also discussed ways to augment the Oracle supplied messages and even provided a Windows based *oerr* implementation.

Common tasks, such as starting and stopping the database, were explored, along with the *oraenv* utility, which sets the Oracle environment on UNIX hosts. Finally, for those DBAs who need to grant SYSDBA and SYSOPER to other users, the *orapwd* utility is available for all platforms.

The next chapter will discuss the data movement utilities – primarily import, export and SQL*Loader.

Chapter 4

Data Copy Utilities

This chapter focuses on utilities that copy data. Data can be copied in many different ways.

First, data can be exported from within Oracle to outside of Oracle (export). Second, data can be imported from outside of the database to inside the database (SQL*Loader). Data can also be copied from one database to another (export/import or SQL*Plus *copy* command) as depicted in Figure 4.1.

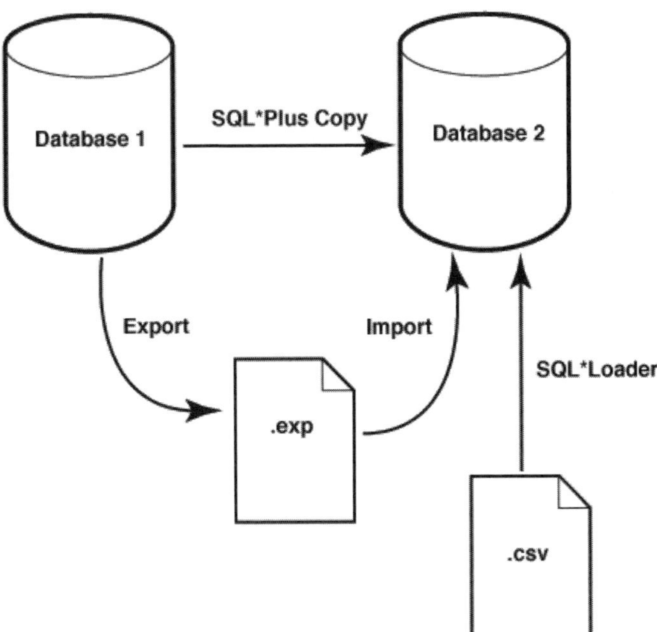

Figure 4.1 – Data Copy Utilities

Choosing the appropriate method for copying data from a source to a destination requires knowledge of the strengths and weaknesses of each data copy utility. Depending on the job at hand, one method may be more suitable than another. This chapter will explain each of the data copy utilities to help make the choice easier.

Throughout this chapter, certain benchmark tests are used. These tests all include the same table, the table with one million rows.

```
SQL> desc table_with_one_million_rows;

 Name                                      Null?    Type
 ----------------------------------------- -------- ------------
 COL1                                                NUMBER
 COL2                                                NUMBER
 COL3                                                VARCHAR2(80)
 COL4                                                VARCHAR2(80)
 COL5                                                VARCHAR2(80)
 COL6                                                DATE
```

The tests were conducted in a single environment running Oracle 9.2 and Windows XP, with an 8K Oracle blocksize. The same tests should be performed in your environment in order to confirm the results. Environmental attributes, such as data types, I/O layout, block sizes, file systems, etc., can impact the results.

Export

The export utility (*exp*) enables DBAs to extract information from the database. Exports play a vital role in a backup and recovery strategy, and are a convenient way to duplicate production data in test environments.

They are used for many reasons, including:

- Logical database backups.
- Copying data from one database to another (used in combination with import).
- Reorganization of segments (utilizing *compress=y*).

The export utility extracts objects (along with their dependent objects) and their data from the database and writes the data to an export file. This file is in binary format and can reside either on disk or tape.

Exporting to disk is much faster, but may not be an option for large databases where free disk space is limited. The export files are only used by the import utility to load the data into a different database or back into the same one. The version of the import utility cannot be older than the export version used.

Export Modes

There are four data export modes:

- **Full** – exports the contents of the entire database. This can be time consuming and requires substantial disk space, depending on the size of the database.

- **User** – exports all objects within a particular schema. If user SCOTT performs a user mode export, all of the objects belonging to SCOTT will be exported.

- **Table** – exports the DDL and data (optional) of any listed tables, table partitions, or subpartitions. If the table specified is partitioned, then all of its partitions will be exported. Table names can be specified using wildcard characters. In the example below, all of user DAVE's tables will be exported, along with any table owned by SCOTT that contains a 'D', and any table owned by AARON that contains an 'S' in the table name.

```
TABLES=(scott.%D%,dave.%,aaron.%S%)
```

- **Tablespace** – exports all the tables residing in the specified tablespace(s). All indexes on the corresponding tables will also be exported, regardless of their tablespace (which should always be a different one than the table). If a table has one partition stored in the specified tablespace, the entire table (all partitions) will be exported. This option requires the *exp_full_database* role.

Each export mode addresses a different requirement and should be used appropriately. For instance, full exports should not be performed when only a few schemas have the data that needs to be exported.

Export Options

In addition to export modes, the export utility enables the user to specify runtime parameters interactively, on the command line, or defined in a parameter file (PARFILE). These options include:

- ***buffer*** – Specifies the size, in bytes, of the buffer used to fetch the rows. If 0 is specified, only one row is fetched at a time. This parameter only applies to conventional (non direct) exports.

- ***compress*** – When "Y", export will mark the table to be loaded as one extent for the import utility. If "N", the current storage options defined for the table will be used. Although this option is only implemented on import, it can only be specified on export.

- ***consistent*** – [N] Specifies the *set transaction read only* statement for export, ensuring data consistency. This option should be set to "Y" if activity is anticipated while the *exp* command is executing. If 'Y' is set, confirm that there is sufficient undo segment space to avoid the export session getting the ORA-1555 Snapshot too old error.

- ***constraints*** – [Y] Specifies whether table constraints should be exported with table data.

- ***direct*** – [N] Determines whether to use direct or conventional path export. Direct path exports bypass the SQL command, thereby enhancing performance.

- ***feedback*** – [0] Determines how often feedback is displayed. A value of feedback=*n* displays a dot for every *n* rows processed. The display shows all tables exported not individual ones. From the output below, each of the 20 dots represent 50,000 rows, totaling 1 million rows for the table.

```
About to export specified tables via Direct Path ...
. . exporting table    TABLE_WITH_ONE_MILLION_ROWS
....................
1000000 rows exported
```

- ***file*** – The name of the export file. Multiple files can be listed, separated by commas. When export fills the *filesize*, it will begin writing to the next file in the list.

- ***filesize*** – The maximum file size, specified in bytes.

- ***flashback_scn*** – The system change number (SCN) that export uses to enable flashback.

- ***flashback_time*** – Export will discover the SCN that is closest to the specified time. This SCN is used to enable flashback.

- ***full*** – The entire database is exported.

* ***grants*** – [Y] Specifies object grants to export.

* ***help*** – Shows command line options for export.

* ***indexes*** – [Y] Determines whether index definitions are exported. The index data is never exported.

* ***log*** – The filename used by export to write messages. The same messages that appear on the screen are written to this file:

```
Connected to: Oracle9i Enterprise Edition Release 9.2.0.1.0 - Production
With the Partitioning, OLAP and Oracle Data Mining options
JServer Release 9.2.0.1.0 - Production
Export done in WE8MSWIN1252 character set and AL16UTF16 NCHAR character set

About to export specified tables via Direct Path ...
. . exporting table    TABLE_WITH_ONE_MILLION_ROWS    1000000 rows exported
Export terminated successfully without warnings.
```

* ***object_consistent*** – [N] Specifies whether export uses SET TRANSACTION READ ONLY to ensure that the data being exported is consistent.

* ***owner*** – Only the owner's objects will be exported.

* ***parfile*** – The name of the file that contains the export parameter options. This file can be used instead of specifying all the options on the command line for each export.

- ***query*** – Allows a subset of rows from a table to be exported, based on a SQL *where* clause (discussed later in this chapter).

- ***recordlength*** – Specifies the length of the file record in bytes. This parameter affects the amount of data that accumulates before it is written to disk. If not specified, this parameter defaults to the value specific to that platform. The highest value is 64KB.

- ***resumable*** – [N] Enables and disables resumable space allocation. When "Y", the parameters *resumable_name* and *resumable_timeout* are utilized.

- ***resumable_name*** – User defined string that helps identify a resumable statement that has been suspended. This parameter is ignored unless *resumable* = *Y*.

- ***resumable_timeout*** – [7200 seconds] The time period in which an export error must be fixed. This parameter is ignored unless *resumable* = *Y*.

- ***rows*** – [Y] Indicates whether or not the table rows should be exported.

- ***statistics*** – [ESTIMATE] Indicates the level of statistics generated when the data is imported. Other options include COMPUTE and NONE.

- ***tables*** – Indicates that the type of export is table-mode and lists the tables to be exported. Table partitions and sub partitions can also be specified.

- ***tablespaces*** – Indicates that the type of export is tablespace-mode, in which all tables assigned to the listed tablespaces will be exported. This option requires the EXP_FULL_DATABASE role.

- ***transport_tablespace*** – [N] Enables the export of metadata needed for transportable tablespaces.

- ***triggers*** – [Y] Indicates whether triggers defined on export tables will also be exported.

- ***tts_full_check*** – [FALSE] When TRUE, export will verify that when creating a transportable tablespace, a consistent set of objects is exported.

- ***userid*** – Specifies the userid/password of the user performing the export.

- ***volsize*** – Specifies the maximum number of bytes in an export file on each tape volume.

The functionality of the export utility has been significantly enhanced in recent versions of Oracle. To check which options are available in any release use:

```
exp help=y
```

Parameter Files

Parameter files are a convenient way to consolidate all the options from a file that will be used when executing the utility. The benefit of the parameter file is that it allows the options to be specified once and reused by all utility jobs. Three of the utilities discussed in this chapter (export, import, SQL*Loader) support parameter files.

Below is an example of an export parameter file: *export_options.par.*

```
compress=n
direct=n
buffer=1000
tables=table_with_one_million_rows
userid=scott/tiger
```

Using this parameter file, the export command line is executed by the following:

```
exp parfile=export_options.par
```

Specifying options in a file makes it much easier to implement the options with any utility that accepts a parameter file. In addition, these options are not revealed on the command line, and therefore not exposed to commands (UNIX *ps* command) that would reveal the username and password had they been specified on the command line.

Exporting Data Subsets

This export utility allows the DBA to limit the number of rows exported, based on a SQL *where* clause. This is very useful when only a portion of the table needs to be exported. For example, to export only those rows from the table whose *order_number* > 873737:

```
QUERY=\"WHERE order_number \> 873737\"
```

The specification of the query text must compensate for special characters that are specific to the operating system. The query text above places the entire string in double quotes and places an escape character (\) in front of special characters. The query specification above would result in the following SQL being executed:

```
select * from orders where order_number > 873737;
```

Subsetting is just one method by which export performance can be improved. The next section discusses other ways to optimize export performance.

Maximizing Export Performance

Many DBAs are faced with the challenge of speeding up utility functions such as export. Typically, an organization has only a small window for maintenance, and utility jobs must complete within that timeframe. Fortunately, there are a few things a DBA can do to expedite exports. These include:

- **Use Direct Path** – Direct path exports (DIRECT=Y) allow the export utility to skip the SQL evaluation buffer, whereas the conventional path export executes SQL SELECT statements. With direct path, the data is read from disk into the buffer cache, returning rows directly to the export client. This can offer substantial performance gains, depending on the actual data. When using the direct path, the *recordlength* parameter should also be used to optimize performance.

- **Use Subsets** – By subsetting the data using the QUERY option, the export process is only executed against the data that needs to be exported. If tables have old rows that are never updated, the old data should be exported once, and from that point only the newer data subsets should be exported. Subsets cannot be specified with direct path exports since SQL is necessary to create the subset.

- **Use a Larger Buffer** – For conventional path exports, a larger buffer will increase the number of rows that are processed between each physical write to the export file. Fewer physical writes equals greater performance. The following formula can be used to determine a proper buffer size:

```
buffer size = rows in array * max row size
```

- **Separate Tables** – Separate those tables that require *consistent=y* from those that don't, in order to expedite the export. This way, the performance penalty will only be incurred for those tables that actually require it.

For the table with one million rows, the following benchmark tests were performed using the different export options.

Export Type	Elapsed Time (seconds)	Time Reduction
conventional	55	-
buffer=2800000	50	9%
direct = y	55	0 %
direct = y recordlength = 50000	41	25%

Table 4.1 - Benchmark tests performed using the different export options.

The table above reveals a small improvement in performance was obtained by increasing the buffer size on a conventional export. Using *direct=y* offered no performance boost over conventional, until it was accompanied by *recordlength*, which reduced the elapsed time by 25 percent.

Once data has been successfully copied to an export file, it can then be used by the import utility, as described in the next section.

Import

The import utility (*imp*) reads files generated by the export utility and loads the objects and data into the database. Tables are created, their data is loaded, and the indexes are built. Following these objects, triggers are imported, constraints are enabled, and bitmap indexes are created.

This sequence is appropriate for a number of reasons. First, rows are inserted before triggers are enabled to prevent the firing of the triggers for each new row. Constraints are loaded last due to referential integrity relationships and dependencies among tables. If each EMPLOYEE row required a valid DEPT row and no rows were in the DEPT table, errors would occur. If both of these tables already existed, the constraints should be disabled during the import and enabled after import – for the same reason.

Import Options

The import modes are the same as the export modes (Full, User, Table, Tablespace) previously described. Imports support the following options:

- ***buffer*** – Specifies the size, in bytes, of the buffer used to insert the data.

- ***commit***– [N] Specifies whether import should *commit* after each array insert. By default, import commits after each table is loaded, however, this can be quite taxing on the rollback segments or undo space for extremely large tables.

- ***compile***– [Y] Tells import to compile procedural objects as they are imported.
- ***constraints*** – [Y] Specifies whether table constraints should also be imported with table data.
- ***datafiles*** – Used only with *transport_tablespace*. This parameter lists datafiles to be transported to the database.
- ***destroy*** – [N] Determines if existing datafiles should be reused. A value of Y will cause import to include the reuse option in the datafile clause of the *create tablespace* statement.
- ***feedback*** – [0] Determines how often feedback is displayed. A value of *feedback=10* displays a dot for every 10 rows processed. This option applies to the total tables imported, not individual ones. Another way to measure the number of rows that have been processed is to execute the following query while the import is active:

```
select rows_processed
  from v$sqlarea
  where  sql_text like 'INSERT %INTO "%'
    and  command_type  = 2
    and  open_versions > 0;
```

* ***file*** – The name of the export file to import. Multiple files can be listed, separated by commas. When export reaches the *filesize* it will begin writing to the next file in the list.

* ***filesize*** – The maximum file size, specified in bytes.

* ***fromuser*** – A comma delimited list of schemas from which to import. If the export file contains many users or even the entire database, the *fromuser* option enables only a subset of those objects (and data) to be imported.

* ***full*** – The entire export file is imported.

* ***grants*** - [Y] Specifies to import object grants.

* ***help*** – Shows command line options for import.

* ***ignore*** – [N] Specifies how object creation errors should be handled. If a table already exists and *ignore=y*, then the rows are imported to the existing tables, otherwise errors will be reported and no rows are loaded into the table.

* ***indexes*** – [Y] Determines whether indexes are imported.

* ***indexfile*** – Specifies a filename that contains index creation statements. This file can be

used to build the indexes after the import has completed.

- ***log*** – The filename used by import to write messages.

- ***parfile*** – The name of the file that contains the import parameter options. This file can be used instead of specifying all the options on the command line.

- ***recordlength*** – Specifies the length of the file record in bytes. This parameter is only used when transferring export files between operating systems that use different default values.

- ***resumable*** – [N] Enables and disables resumable space allocation. When "Y", the parameters *resumable_name* and *resumable_timeout* are utilized.

- ***resumable_name*** – User defined string that helps identify a resumable statement that has been suspended. This parameter is ignored unless *resumable* = *Y*.

- ***resumable_timeout*** – [7200 seconds] The time period in which an error must be fixed. This parameter is ignored unless *resumable*=*Y*.

- ***rows*** – [Y] Indicates whether or not the table rows should be imported.

- ***show*** – [N] When *show=y*, the DDL within the export file is displayed.

- ***skip_unusable_indexes*** – [N] Determines whether import skips the building of indexes that are in an unusable state.

- ***statistics*** – [ALWAYS] Determines the level of optimizer statistics that are generated on import. The options include ALWAYS, NONE, SAFE and RECALCULATE. ALWAYS imports statistics regardless of their validity. NONE does not import or recalculate any optimizer statistics. SAFE will import the statistics if they appear to be valid, otherwise they will be recomputed after import. RECALCULATE always generates new statistics after import.

- ***streams_configuration*** – [Y] Determines whether or not any streams metadata present in the export file will be imported.

- ***streams_instantiation*** – [N] Specifies whether or not to import streams instantiation metadata present in the export file.

- ***tables*** – Indicates that the type of export is table-mode and lists the tables to be exported. Table partitions and sub partitions can also be specified.

- ***tablespaces*** – When *transport_tablespace=y*, this parameter provides a list of tablespaces.

- ***toid_novalidate*** – Specifies whether or not type validation should occur on import. Import compares the type's unique ID (TOID) with the ID stored in the export file. No table rows will be imported if the TOIDs do not match. This parameter can be used to specify types to exclude from TOID comparison.

- ***to_user*** – Specifies a list of user schemas that will be targets for imports.

- ***transport_tablespace*** – [N] When Y, transportable tablespace metadata will be imported from the export file.

- ***tts_owners*** – When *transport_tablespace=Y*, this parameter lists the users who own the data in the transportable tablespace set.

- ***userid*** – Specifies the userid/password of the user performing the import.

- ***volsize*** – Specifies the maximum number of bytes in an export file on each tape volume.

To check which options are available in any release of import use:

```
imp help=y
```

Maximizing Import Performance

The options used when the data is exported have no influence on how the data is imported. For example, it is irrelevant to the import process whether it was a direct path export or not. The result is a plain export file whether is was generated from direct or conventional means.

Unfortunately, there is no *direct* option available for imports (only for export and SQL*loader). The import process has more tuning limitations than other utilities. The DBA should consider the following when trying to optimize import performance:

- **Set *commit=n*** – For tables that can afford not to *commit* until the end of the load, this option provides a significant performance increase. Larger tables may not be suitable for this option due to the required rollback/undo space.

- **Set *indexes=n*** – Index creation can be postponed until after import completes, by specifying *indexes=n.* If indexes for the target table already exist at the time of execution, import performs index maintenance when data is inserted into the table. Setting *indexes=n* eliminates this maintenance overhead.

- **Use the *buffer* parameter** – By using a larger buffer setting, import can do more work before disk access is performed.

When tuning import, emphasize reducing the amount of work that import needs to do. This can be accomplished by committing less frequently, not importing indexes, not generating statistics, or by using the *buffer* parameter to reduce disk access.

For the table with one million rows, the following benchmark tests were performed using the different import options. The table was truncated after each import.

Import Option	Elapsed Time (Seconds)	Time Reduction
commit=y	120	-
commit=y buffer=64000	100	17%
commit=n buffer=30720	72	40%
commit=N buffer = 64000	67	44%

Table 4.2 - Shows that increasing the size of the buffer has a positive performance impact.

The table above shows that increasing the size of the buffer has a positive performance impact. However, the most dramatic increase in performance was obtained when setting *commit=n*. The increase in the size of the buffer resulted in a marginal improvement when *commit=n*.

Before devising a strategy for using export / import to copy data from one database to another, the SQL*Plus *copy* command should be considered.

The SQL*Plus *copy* Utility

The SQL*Plus COPY command can copy data between two databases via SQL*Net. The preferred method of doing this is to use SQL*Plus on the host where the database resides. If performing the *copy* command from a client SQL*Net connection, the data is transferred through the client machine.

The *copy* command copies data from one Oracle instance to another. The data is simply copied directly from a source to a target. The format of the copy command is:

```
COPY FROM database TO database action -
  destination_table (column_name, column_name...) USING query
```

The action can include:

- ***create*** – If the destination table already exists, *copy* will report an error, otherwise the table is created and the data is copied.
- ***replace*** – If the destination table exists, *copy* will drop and recreate the table with the newly copied data. Otherwise, it will create the table and populate it with the data.
- ***insert*** – If the destination table exists, *copy* inserts the new rows into the table. Otherwise, *copy* reports an error and aborts.

* ***append***– Inserts the data into the table if it exists, otherwise it will create the table and then insert the data.

```
SQL> copy from scott/tiger@ORCL92 -
     to scott/tiger@ORCL92-
     create new_emp -
     using select * from emp;
```

Once the command above is executed, the *copy* utility displays the values of three parameters, each of which can be set with the SQL*Plus *set* command. The *arraysize* specifies the number of rows that SQL*Plus will retrieve from the database at one time. The *copycommit* parameter specifies how often a *commit* is performed and is related to the number of trips – one trip is the number of rows defined in *arraysize*. Finally, the *long* parameter displays the maximum number of characters copied for each column with a LONG datatype.

```
Array fetch/bind size is 15. (arraysize is 15)
Will commit when done. (copycommit is 0)
Maximum long size is 80. (long is 80)
Table NEW_EMP created.

   1400 rows selected from scott@ORCL92.
   1400 rows inserted into NEW_EMP.
   1400 rows committed into NEW_EMP at scott@ORCL92.

SQL> desc new_emp;

 Name                                      Null?    Type
 ----------------------------------------- -------- --------------
 EMPNO                                     NOT NULL NUMBER(4)
 ENAME                                              VARCHAR2(10)
 JOB                                                VARCHAR2(9)
 MGR                                                NUMBER(4)
 HIREDATE                                           DATE
 SAL                                                NUMBER(7,2)
 COMM                                               NUMBER(7,2)
 DEPTNO                                             NUMBER(2)
```

The command above did not specify column names for the new table (*new_emp*). As a result, the new table will have the same column names as the table being copied. If different column names are required, they can be specified after the table name:

```
create new_emp (col1, col2, …) -
```

However, if one column name is specified, they all must be specified.

A DBA could perform this same function with a database link from one database pointing to another. The appeal of the *copy* command is that it only requires SQL*Net service names and proper privileges to get the job done. For those environments that restrict the usage of database links, the *copy* utility can be leveraged. In addition, the *copy* command provides many options, as defined by the actions create, replace, insert and append.

If the *copy* command is executed from a client PC to copy data from remote database DB0 to remote database DB1, the data will be copied from DB0 to the client PC and then to DB1. For this reason, it is best to use SQL*Plus from either remote host and not require the data to travel through a client machine in order to reach its final destination.

The following command copied the *table_with_one_million_rows* table to *new_table*:

```
SQL> copy from scott/tiger@orcl92 -
> to scott/tiger@orcl92 -
> create new_table -
> using select * from table_with_one_million_rows;

Array fetch/bind size is 5000. (arraysize is 5000)
Will commit after every 5000 array binds. (copycommit is 5000)
Maximum long size is 80. (long is 80)
Table NEW_TABLE created.

   1000000 rows selected from scott@orcl92.
   1000000 rows inserted into NEW_TABLE.
   1000000 rows committed into NEW_TABLE at scott@orcl92.
```

The elapsed time for this *copy* command was consistently 85 seconds. However, there was no network involved in this test since the command created the new table in the same instance. The next utility described as SQL*Loader, provides the ability to load data from ASCII (flat) files into the database with great speed.

SQL*Loader

SQL*Loader (*sqlldr*) is the utility to use for high performance data loads. The data can be loaded from any text file and inserted into the database.

Figure 4.2 depicts the SQL*Loader architecture. SQL*Loader reads a data file and a description of the data which is defined in the control file. Using this information and any additional specified parameters (either on the command line or in the PARFILE), SQL*Loader loads the data into the database.

During processing, SQL*Loader writes messages to the log file, bad rows to the bad file, and discarded rows to the discard file.

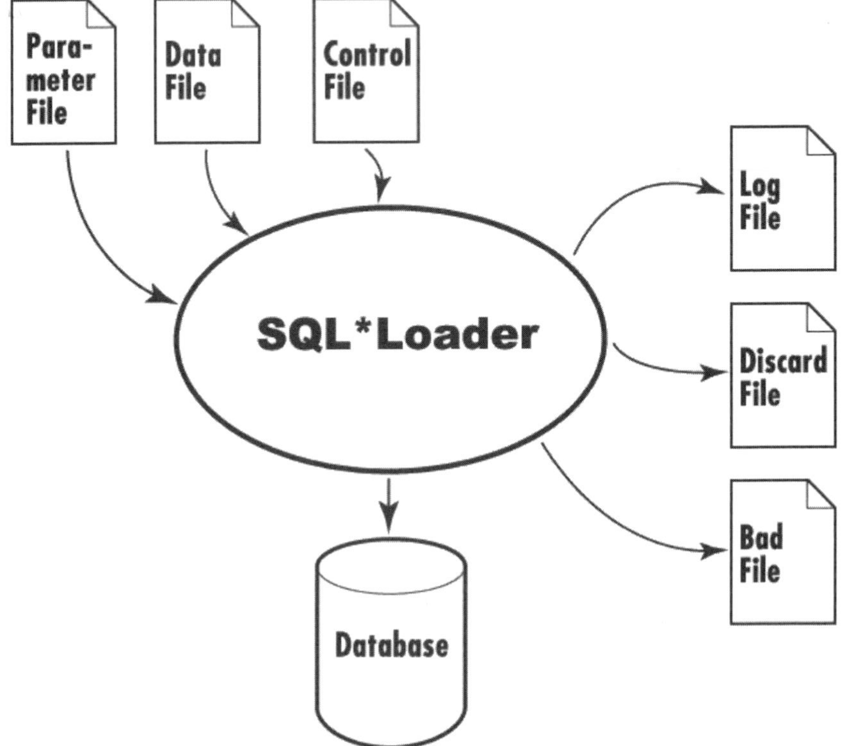

*Figure 4.2 – SQL*Loader Architecture*

The Control File

The SQL*Loader control file contains information that describes how the data will be loaded. It contains the table name, column datatypes, field delimiters, etc. It simply provides the guts for all SQL*Loader processing.

Manually creating control files is an error-prone process. The following SQL script (*controlfile.sql*) can be used to generate an accurate control file for a given table. The script accepts a table name and a date format (to be used for date columns), and generates a valid control file to use with SQL*Loader for that table.

controlfile.sql

```
set echo off ver off feed off pages 0
accept tname prompt 'Enter Name of Table: '
accept dformat prompt 'Enter Format to Use for Date Columns: '

spool &tname..ctl

select 'LOAD DATA'|| chr (10) ||
       'INFILE ''' || lower (table_name) || '.dat''' || chr (10) ||
       'INTO TABLE '|| table_name || chr (10)||
       'FIELDS TERMINATED BY '','''||chr (10)||
       'TRAILING NULLCOLS' || chr (10) || '('
from   user_tables
where  table_name = upper ('&tname');

select decode (rownum, 1, '   ', ' , ') ||
       rpad (column_name, 33, ' ')      ||
       decode (data_type,
           'VARCHAR2', 'CHAR NULLIF ('||column_name||'=BLANKS)',
           'FLOAT',    'DECIMAL EXTERNAL
NULLIF('||column_name||'=BLANKS)',
           'NUMBER',   decode (data_precision, 0,
                       'INTEGER EXTERNAL NULLIF ('||column_name||
                       '=BLANKS)', decode (data_scale, 0,
                       'INTEGER EXTERNAL NULLIF ('||
                       column_name||'=BLANKS)',
                       'DECIMAL EXTERNAL NULLIF ('||
                       column_name||'=BLANKS)')),
           'DATE',     'DATE "&dformat" NULLIF
('||column_name||'=BLANKS)', null)
from   user_tab_columns
where  table_name = upper ('&tname')
order  by column_id;

select ')'
from dual;
spool off
```

Once executed and given a table name and date format, *controlfile.sql* will generate a control file with the following contents:

controlfile.par

```
LOAD DATA
INFILE 'table_with_one_million_rows.dat'
INTO TABLE TABLE_WITH_ONE_MILLION_ROWS
FIELDS TERMINATED BY ','
TRAILING NULLCOLS
(
   COL1                        DECIMAL EXTERNAL NULLIF (COL1=BLANKS)
 , COL2                        DECIMAL EXTERNAL NULLIF (COL2=BLANKS)
 , COL3                        CHAR NULLIF (COL3=BLANKS)
 , COL4                        CHAR NULLIF (COL4=BLANKS)
 , COL5                        CHAR NULLIF (COL5=BLANKS)
 , COL6                        DATE "MM-DD-YYYY" NULLIF (COL6=BLANKS)
)
```

The control file can also specify that records are in fixed format. A file is in fixed record format when all records in a datafile are the same length. The control file specifies the specific starting and ending byte location of each field. This format is harder to create and less flexible but can yield performance benefits. A control file specifying a fixed format for the same table could look like the following:

```
LOAD DATA
INFILE 'table_with_one_million_rows.dat'
INTO TABLE TABLE_WITH_ONE_MILLION_ROWS
(
   COL1  POSITION(1:4)      INTEGER EXTERNAL
 , COL2  POSITION(6:9)      INTEGER EXTERNAL
 , COL3  POSITION(11:46)    CHAR
 , col4  position(48:83)    CHAR
 , col5  position(85:120)   CHAR
 , COL6  POSITION(122:130)  DATE "MMDDYYYY"
 )
```

The Log File

The log file contains information about the SQL*loader execution. It should be viewed after each SQL*Loader job is complete. Especially interesting is the summary information at the bottom of the log, including CPU time and elapsed time. The data below is a sample of the contents of the log file.

```
*************************************************************************************************
SQL*Loader: Release 9.2.0.1.0 - Production on Mon Mar 10 23:39:04 2003

Copyright (c) 1982, 2002, Oracle Corporation.  All rights reserved.

*************************************************************************************************
Control File:   sqlload.par
Data File:      sqlload.txt
  Bad File:     sqlload.bad
  Discard File:  none specified

 (Allow all discards)

Number to load: ALL
Number to skip: 0
Errors allowed: 50
Continuation:    none specified
Path used:      Direct

Table TABLE_WITH_ONE_MILLION_ROWS, loaded from every logical record.
Insert option in effect for this table: INSERT
TRAILING NULLCOLS option in effect

Table TABLE_WITH_ONE_MILLION_ROWS, loaded from every logical record.
Insert option in effect for this table: INSERT
TRAILING NULLCOLS option in effect

   Column Name                  Position   Len  Term Encl Datatype
------------------------------ ---------- ----- ---- ---- ---------
COL1                                FIRST     *   ,       CHARACTER
    NULL if COL1 = BLANKS
COL2                                 NEXT     *   ,       CHARACTER
    NULL if COL2 = BLANKS
COL3                                 NEXT     *   ,       CHARACTER
    NULL if COL3 = BLANKS
COL4                                 NEXT     *   ,       CHARACTER
    NULL if COL4 = BLANKS
COL5                                 NEXT     *   ,       CHARACTER
    NULL if COL5 = BLANKS
COL6                                 NEXT     *   ,       DATE MMDDYYYY
    NULL if COL6 = BLANKS


Table TABLE_WITH_ONE_MILLION_ROWS:
  1000000 Rows successfully loaded.
  0 Rows not loaded due to data errors.
  0 Rows not loaded because all WHEN clauses were failed.
  0 Rows not loaded because all fields were null.

  Date cache:
   Max Size:      1000
   Entries :         1
   Hits    :    999999
   Misses  :         0

Bind array size not used in direct path.
Column array  rows :    5000
Stream buffer bytes:  512000
Read   buffer bytes: 1048576

Total logical records skipped:          0
Total logical records read:       1000000
Total logical records rejected:         0
Total logical records discarded:        0
Total stream buffers loaded by SQL*Loader main thread:      255
Total stream buffers loaded by SQL*Loader load thread:      128

Run began on Mon Mar 10 23:39:04 2003
```

```
Run ended on Mon Mar 10 23:39:51 2003

Elapsed time was:     00:00:47.55
CPU time was:         00:00:12.85
```

SQL*Loader Options

SQL*Loader provides the following options, which can be specified either on the command line or within a parameter file:

- ***bad*** – A file that is created when at least one record from the input file is rejected. The rejected data records are placed in this file. A record could be rejected for many reasons, including a non-unique key or a required column being null.

- ***bindsize*** – [256000] The size of the bind array in bytes.

- ***columnarrayrows*** – [5000] Specifies the number of rows to allocate for direct path column arrays.

- ***control*** – The name of the control file. This file specifies the format of the data to be loaded.

- ***data*** – The name of the file that contains the data to load.

- ***direct*** – [FALSE] Specifies whether or not to use a direct path load or conventional load.

- ***discard*** – The name of the file that contains the discarded rows. Discarded rows are those that fail the WHEN clause condition when selectively loading records.

- ***discardmax*** – [ALL] The maximum number of discards to allow.

- ***errors*** – [50] The number of errors to allow on the load.

- ***external_table*** – [NOT_USED] Determines whether or not any data will be loaded using external tables. The other valid options include GENERATE_ONLY and EXECUTE.

- ***file*** – Used only with parallel loads, this parameter specifies the file to allocate extents from.

- ***load*** – [ALL] The number of logical records to load.

- ***log*** – The name of the file used by SQL*Loader to log results.

- ***multithreading*** – The default is TRUE on multiple CPU systems and FALSE on single CPU systems.

- ***parfile*** – [Y] The name of the file that contains the parameter options for SQL*Loader.

- ***parallel*** – [FALSE] Specifies a filename that contains index creation statements.

- ***readsize*** – The size of the buffer used by SQL*Loader when reading data from the input file. This value should match that of *bindsize.*

- ***resumable*** – [N] Enables and disables resumable space allocation. When "Y", the parameters *resumable_name* and *resumable_timeout* are utilized.

- ***resumable_name*** – User defined string that helps identify a resumable statement that has been suspended. This parameter is ignored unless *resumable* = *Y*.

- ***resumable_timeout*** – [7200 seconds] The time period in which an error must be fixed. This parameter is ignored unless *resumable* = *Y*.

- ***rows*** – [64] The number of rows to load before a *commit* is issued (conventional path only). For direct path loads, rows are the number of rows to read from the data file before saving the data in the datafiles.

- ***silent*** – Suppress errors during data load. A value of ALL will suppress all load messages. Other options include DISCARDS, ERRORS, FEEDBACK, HEADER, and PARTITIONS.

- ***skip*** – [0] Allows the skipping of the specified number of logical records.

- ***skip_unusable_indexes*** – [FALSE] Determines whether SQL*Loader skips the building of indexes that are in an unusable state.

- ***skip_index_maintenance*** – [FALSE] Stops index maintenance for direct path loads only.

- ***streamsize*** – [256000] Specifies the size of direct path streams in bytes.

- ***userid*** – The Oracle username and password.

To check which options are available in any release of SQL*Loader use this command:

```
sqlldr help=y
```

Maximizing SQL*Loader Performance

SQL*Loader is flexible and offers many options that should be considered to maximize the speed of data loads. These include:

- **Use Direct Path Loads** - The conventional path loader essentially loads the data by using standard insert statements. The direct path loader (*direct=true*) loads directly into the Oracle data files and creates blocks in Oracle database block format. The fact that SQL is not being issued makes the entire process much less taxing on the database. There are certain cases, however, in which direct path loads cannot be used (clustered tables). To prepare the database for direct path loads, the script *$ORACLE_HOME/rdbms/admin/catldr.sql.sql* must be executed.

- **Disable Indexes and Constraints.** For conventional data loads only, the disabling of indexes and constraints can greatly enhance the performance of SQL*Loader.

- **Use a Larger Bind Array**. For conventional data loads only, larger bind arrays limit the number of calls to the database and increase performance. The size of the bind array is specified using the *bindsize* parameter. The bind array's size is equivalent to the number of rows it contains (*rows=*) times the maximum length of each row.

- **Use ROWS=*n* to Commit Less Frequently.** For conventional data loads only, the *rows* parameter specifies the number of rows per *commit.* Issuing fewer commits will enhance performance.

- **Use Parallel Loads.** Available with direct path data loads only, this option allows multiple SQL*Loader jobs to execute concurrently.

```
$ sqlldr control=first.ctl  parallel=true direct=true
$ sqlldr control=second.ctl parallel=true direct=true
```

- **Use Fixed Width Data.** Fixed width data format saves Oracle some processing when parsing the data. The savings can be tremendous, depending on the type of data and number of rows.

- **Disable Archiving During Load.** While this may not be feasible in certain environments, disabling database archiving can increase performance considerably.

- **Use *unrecoverable*.** The unrecoverable option (unrecoverable load data) disables the writing of the data to the redo logs. This option is available for direct path loads only.

Using the table *table_with_one_million_rows*, the following benchmark tests were performed with the various SQL*Loader options. The table was truncated after each test.

SQL*Loader Option	Elapsed Time (Seconds)	Time Reduction
direct=false rows=64	135	-
direct=false bindsize=512000 rows=10000	92	32%
direct=false bindsize=512000 rows=10000 database in noarchivelog mode	85	37%
direct=true	47	65%
direct=true unrecoverable	41	70%

SQL*Loader Option	Elapsed Time (Seconds)	Time Reduction
direct=true unrecoverable fixed width data	41	70%

Table 4.3 – Results indicate conventional path loads take longest.

The results above indicate that conventional path loads take the longest. However, the *bindsize* and *rows* parameters can aid the performance under these loads. The test involving the conventional load didn't come close to the performance of the direct path load with the *unrecoverable* option specified.

It is also worth noting that the fastest import time achieved for this table (earlier) was 67 seconds, compared to 41 for SQL*Loader direct path – a 39% reduction in execution time. This proves that SQL*Loader can load the same data faster than import.

These tests did not compensate for indexes. All database load operations will execute faster when indexes are disabled.

External Tables in 9i

In version 9, Oracle introduced the concept of external tables. These objects provide a way to access data stored outside of the database with a SQL statement. These also provide an alternative to SQL*Loader, given their simplicity and comparable performance. Data loads can be performed by simple statements like:

```
SQL> create table load_table as select * from external_table;
```

When executed, the data would be loaded from an operating system data file into *LOAD_TABLE*.

Summary

The data copy utilities are some of the most useful utilities within Oracle. This chapter gave a high level overview of each utility, with an emphasis on optimizing them in specific environments. Each utility supports a number of options, many more than could be detailed in this chapter.

Performance is always an issue with the data copy utilities. The best way to optimize performance of any of these utilities is to eliminate any steps that are not required. In addition, it is clear from the performance benchmarks that the *direct* option should be utilized for any utility that supports it. However, it is important to note that direct path exports are different than direct path SQL*Loader executions. A direct path export simply skips the SQL evaluation buffer, whereas a direct path load writes directly to the Oracle datafiles.

The best export time achieved for the benchmark was 41 seconds. The best import time was 67 seconds, for a total export/import elapsed time of 108 seconds. The *copy* command copied the same table data to a new table in the same database in 85 seconds using SQL*Net! The *copy* command is indeed a viable option for copying data from one database to another.

SQL*Loader is hard to beat for fast data loads, especially when using direct path loads and the *unrecoverable* option. If only SQL*Loader worked with an export file, it would greatly enhance the entire unload/load process.

The next chapter will discuss those utilities that aid the DBA in monitoring and tuning the Oracle environment.

Chapter 5

Monitoring and Tuning

Expert DBAs are constantly looking for tools that assist them in doing their job more effectively. Fortunately, many good tools exist right there in the bin directory of every Oracle installation or in the database itself in the form of a DBMS supplied package.

This chapter will discuss those utilities that aid a DBA in monitoring and tuning their environment. Some of these utilities are space-related while others apply to tuning SQL. There is another utility that provides a very useful way for the Oracle database to communicate alerts to the DBA.

The utilities covered in this chapter include dbms_alert, utl_smtp, oemctl, dbverify, dbms_xplan, and dbms_repair.

The first utility described in this chapter enables the database to send events to client machines – *dbms_alert.*

The *dbms_alert* Utility

The *dbms_alert* package was first available in Oracle 7 and is rarely used. Oracle is such a vast and complicated set of software components that it is virtually impossible to stay current on all of its features and capabilities.

The *dbms_alert* package provides an alerting mechanism based on events. An event can be defined as an occurrence, or an action. Example events include the payroll table being updated, a specific user logging on to the database, or available free space less than 20 MB. Anything that is detectable can be used to trigger an event.

The package has an asynchronous communication infrastructure but the DBA uses the utility to assign messages their content. DBAs can use it for database monitoring and application developers can use it to signal business or application events.

The *dbms_alert* package is created by executing the *catproc.sql* file and is owned by SYS. Once granted the execute privilege to *dbms_alert*, it can be executed by any software component that can call a stored procedure including SQL*Plus, Java and Pro*C.

The *dbms_alert* package provides a mechanism for the database to notify a client (anything listening) of an event asynchronously, which means that the application does not need to periodically check for the occurrence of events. Instead, when an event occurs, a notification will be sent. In the past, developers created a polling process that checked the status of something on the database, like a completed job, by checking for a table value that the process had just updated. *dbms_alert* renders such techniques obsolete and is one of the best Oracle supplied packages.

The *dbms_alert* package is even more helpful when dealing with 3 tier web applications – client, web server, and database. Web applications are "stateless" by nature, meaning that the web server processes a request and it's done - there is no tethered connection like we're accustomed to with SQL*Plus, Oracle Applications, or SAP R/3. *dbms_alert* provides a way for the database to initiate contact with the web server, who in turn can notify clients attached to it.

How It Works

The *dbms_alert* package begins with a client process registering interest in an alert. Once it registers for an alert, it waits for that specific alert (*waitone*) or any other alert (*waitany*) to occur. Once the alert occurs, the client is notified and a string is passed containing whatever the signal process selected to send to the client (Figure 5.1).

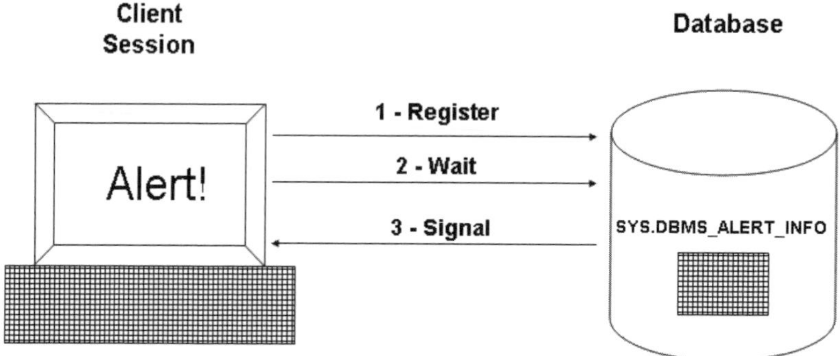

Figure 5.1 – dbms_alert Model

Once the call to *waitone* or *waitany* is made, Oracle will check the *dbms_alert_info* table to see if any new rows have been inserted. If a new row exists, the data in the column *message* is returned from the procedure call.

The Java program below (*Alert.java*) can be executed from the DOS or UNIX prompt. This program prompts for database connection information, connects to the database via JDBC, registers for an alert, and waits for the LOGONALERT alert to occur. It can easily be customized to not only display an event but to prompt for the event of interest.

alert.java

```
import java.sql.*;
import java.io.*;
import java.util.*;
import oracle.jdbc.driver.*;


public class Alert
   {
    static String host, dbname, port, user, password, option = null;
    public static void main(String args[])
    {
     InputStreamReader isr = new InputStreamReader ( System.in );
     BufferedReader br = new BufferedReader ( isr );
     System.out.print("      ************************************************\n");
     System.out.print("      * This is a simple utility to test             *\n");
     System.out.print("      * the alert notification between the database  *\n");
     System.out.print("      * and any client application                   *\n");
     System.out.print("      ************************************************\n\n");


 try {
     System.out.print("                    Enter Host Name: ");
     host = br.readLine();
     System.out.print("\n              Enter Database Name: ");
     dbname = br.readLine();
     System.out.print("\n         Enter TNS Listener Port#: ");
     port = br.readLine();
     System.out.print("\n         Enter Database User Name: ");
     user = br.readLine();
     System.out.print("\n    Enter Database User Password: ");
     password = br.readLine();

     System.out.print("\n Press <Ctrl><C> at any time to exit \n\n");

     DriverManager.registerDriver(new oracle.jdbc.driver.OracleDriver());
     Connection databaseConnection =
         DriverManager.getConnection("jdbc:oracle:thin:@" +
         host + ":" +
         port + ":" +
         dbname, user, password);

      System.out.print("\n\nSuccessully connected to " + dbname + " as " + user);
      System.out.print("\n");

      String sql     = null;
      String message = null;
      String status  = null;

      sql = "{call dbms_alert.register('LOGONALERT')}";
      CallableStatement cs1 = databaseConnection.prepareCall(sql) ;
      cs1.execute();
      sql = "{call dbms_alert.waitone('LOGONALERT', ?, ?)}";

      CallableStatement cs2 = databaseConnection.prepareCall(sql) ;
      cs2.registerOutParameter(1, Types.VARCHAR);
      cs2.registerOutParameter(2, Types.VARCHAR);

      int x = 0;

      while (x==0) {
         cs2.execute();
         String Result = cs2.getString(1);
         System.out.print(Result + "\n");
      }

      databaseConnection.close();

     } // try


     catch (SQLException sqle) {
```

```
        System.out.print("Unable to connect, error: " + sqle );
    }
    catch (IOException ioe) {
        System.out.print("IO Exception (bad data): " + ioe );
    }
  }
}
```

Next, a trigger will be created that will signal this event. The signal code is the key to the trigger below. Notice that it contains the same alert name that the client registered, LOGONALERT.

```
dbms_alert.signal('LOGONALERT', ,<any string we want to send> );
commit;
```

The following PL/SQL (*Logontrigger.sql*) is an AFTER LOGON TRIGGER that sends information to those registered for LOGONALERT. As part of the signal call, it returns the user, machine, and time that the user logged on. The *commit* statement after the signal call is required to send the signal.

logontrigger.sql

```
CREATE or replace TRIGGER on_connect
  AFTER LOGON ON DATABASE
    DECLARE
       pragma autonomous_transaction;  -- needed for trigger commit
       vsess       varchar2(30);
       vuser       varchar2(30);
       vmachine    varchar2(30);
       vosuser     varchar2(30);
       dbname      varchar2(40);
    BEGIN
        select userenv('SESSIONID') into vsess from dual;
        select username, machine, osuser
           into vuser,vmachine,vosuser
           from v$session where audsid = vsess;
        select value
           into dbname
           from v$parameter
           where name = 'db_name';
        dbms_alert.signal('LOGONALERT', 'User: ' || vuser ||
             ' logged on from ' || vmachine ||
             ' at ' || to_char(sysdate,'mm-dd-yyyy HH24:MI:SS'));
        commit;  -- required for the signal to work
    END;
  /
```

Once everything is configured, the trigger will fire when a user connects to the database. From the operating system, the program will be started and the required information entered.

```
C:\oracle9i\bin>java Alert

      *********************************************
      * This is a simple utility to test          *
      * the alert notification between the database *
      * and any client application                *
      *********************************************

                  Enter Host Name: MoorePC

            Enter Database Name: ORCL92

       Enter TNS Listener Port#: 1521

       Enter Database User Name: scott

   Enter Database User Password: tiger


 Press <Ctrl><C> at any time to exit


Successully connected to ORCL92 as scott

User: SYS logged on from WORKGROUP\MOOREPC  at 01-02-2003 21:18:37
```

SCOTT was the user that connected to the database to wait for the event. Within one second of user SCOTT logging in to the database, the LOGINALERT was signaled and sent to the Java client. Based on the message above, the SYS user logged in to the database.

Duplicating this Java code functionality in SQL*Plus would be simple, although not as functional, since SQL*Plus is not automatically notified of the event. The print statement below is used to check the status of the logon alert message.

```
SQL> var out1 varchar2(800)
SQL> var out2 varchar2(800)
SQL> exec dbms_alert.waitone('LOGONALERT', :out1, :out2);
PL/SQL procedure successfully completed.

SQL> print out1

OUT1
--------------------------------------------------------------------------
User: SYS logged on from WORKGROUP\MOOREPC  at 01-02-2003 21:24:55
```

The *dbms_alert_info* Table

Any alert that has been registered via *dbms_alert.register* is inserted into the *dbms_alert_info* table. This table is owned by the SYS user and contains the data for registered alerts. A DBA can query this table to discover who is waiting for certain events. This can be important since the DBA may want to inspect the types of alerts that are being generated. In addition, in the event that the database needs restarting, the DBA can see the sessions waiting on events that will be impacted.

The columns of the *dbms_alert_info* table include:

- ***Name*** - The name of the alert specified by the user.
- ***SID*** – Session ID of the session that is waiting for this alert.
- ***Changed*** – Y/N indicator that the alert has been signaled. Y = alert signaled, N = no alert signaled via (*dbms_alert.SIGNAL*)
- ***Message*** – An 800-byte character string that can be passed to the client waiting for the

alert. An 800-byte character is large enough to send a meaningful message to any registered client. This message is optional, since the occurrence of a specific alert may be enough information alone.

dbms_alert Methods

The following options are available when utilizing *dbms_alert*. The *register* and *signal* procedures are required, the rest are optional.

- ***register*** – The register procedure adds a session and specified alert to a registration list that appears in the *dbms_alert_info* table. There is no limit to the number of alerts a session can register. When the session is no longer interested in receiving alerts, the remove procedure (or *remove_all*) should be called to deactivate the notifications. Register always performs a *commit* on exit.

- ***remove*** – Procedure that removes the specified alert from the registration list for a particular session. This should always be called when the session is no longer interested in receiving particular alerts.

- ***remove_all*** – Procedure that removes all of the registered events for that session.

- ***set_defaults*** – This procedure sets the default polling interval, in seconds.

- ***signal*** - The signal procedure sends an alert to any session that has registered for it. The signal includes the name of the alert along with an optional 800-character string. This string negates the need for client sessions to ping the database for information. The SIGNAL only works after a *commit* is issued.

- ***waitany*** – In the event that a session has registered interest in many alerts, the *waitany* procedure is used for the client to be notified if any of them occur. *Waitany* avoids the need to implement multiple *waitone* calls, thereby simplifying the code. When *waitany* is called, the timeout period in seconds can be specified.

- ***waitone*** – This procedure waits for one alert to occur as specified in the call to *waitone.*

Practical Uses for *dbms_alert*

There are many times that users would prefer instant notification. For a DBA, the following events may prove worthy of real-time alerts:

- Unauthorized users logging on to database

- Unauthorized table access

- Performance measurements, including long wait events and locks

- Free space deficit

- Queries that have exceeded n seconds in CPU usage

The *dbms_alert* package is a powerful tool that allows asynchronous notification of events. Any event the DBA chooses can be monitored and communicated to any client application that registers an interest in the event. The *dbms_alert* package is a great tool that enhances the monitoring skills of the DBA.

The next utility describes how to send e-mail alerts from the database.

The *utl_smtp* Utility

The *utl_smtp* utility enables e-mail messages to be sent from the database (PL/SQL) to any valid e-mail address. This can be very useful in database monitoring since e-mails can be sent to production support personnel when certain events occur. These events could be anything ranging from space deficits to unauthorized database access. Anything that can be monitored can be sent in an e-mail.

The procedure below (*sendmail.sql*) provides simple e-mail capability. It requires an SMTP host port (25) to be opened. The host can be specified by host name or IP address, with 127.0.0.1 representing the local host machine. Once the port is opened, the procedure specifies the subject, sender, recipient and body of the message.

sendmail.sql

```
CREATE OR REPLACE PROCEDURE SEND_MAIL (
  msg_to      varchar2,
  msg_subject varchar2,
  msg_text    varchar2   )
IS
  c  utl_smtp.connection;
  rc integer;
  msg_from    varchar2(50) := 'Oracle9.2';
  mailhost    VARCHAR2(30) := '127.0.0.1';   -- local database host

BEGIN
  c := utl_smtp.open_connection(mailhost, 25); -- SMTP on port 25
  utl_smtp.helo(c, mailhost);
  utl_smtp.mail(c, msg_from);
  utl_smtp.rcpt(c, msg_to);

  utl_smtp.data(c,'From: Oracle Database' || utl_tcp.crlf ||
                        'To: ' || msg_to || utl_tcp.crlf ||
                        'Subject: ' || msg_subject ||
                         utl_tcp.crlf || msg_text);
  utl_smtp.quit(c);

  EXCEPTION
    WHEN UTL_SMTP.INVALID_OPERATION THEN
       dbms_output.put_line(' Invalid Operation in Mail attempt
                              using UTL_SMTP.');
    WHEN UTL_SMTP.TRANSIENT_ERROR THEN
       dbms_output.put_line(' Temporary e-mail issue - try again');
    WHEN UTL_SMTP.PERMANENT_ERROR THEN
       dbms_output.put_line(' Permanent Error Encountered.');
END;
/
```

Calling the sendmail procedure can be performed like below:

```
exec send_mail(msg_to=>'dave@oracleutilities.com', -
               msg_subject => 'Hello from Oracle', -
               msg_text    => 'This is the body of the message'-
            );
```

The e-mail will be sent from the database and received by the recipient. Figure 5.2 displays the actual e-mail as delivered to my inbox.

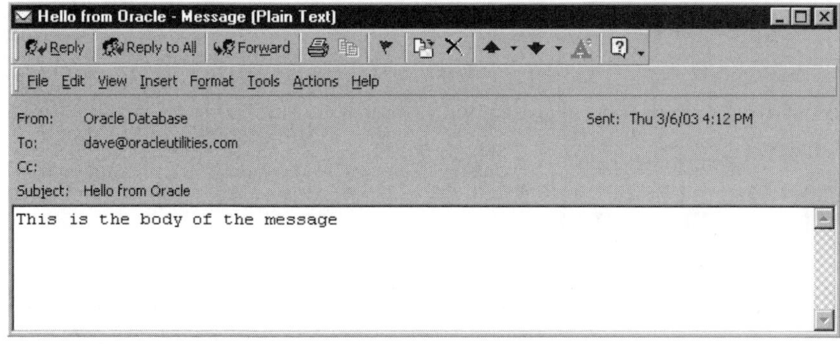

Figure 5.2 – Email Received From Oracle

E-mail is a powerful feature that can enhance any monitoring environment. E-mails can be sent from any PL/SQL code to any valid e-mail address including wireless devices that are e-mail enabled. Database content can be included in the body of the message thereby giving the DBA all of the information they need to resolve the problem. The following events are certainly worthy of an e-mail when they occur:

- A tablespace running out of space
- The archive destination directory running out of space
- An object unable to allocate the next extent
- Unauthorized access to, or within, the database
- A query taking *n* seconds of CPU
- New errors in the alert log

utl_smtp is a powerful utility that should be utilized in a monitoring environment. The next utility described is one used by Oracle Enterprise Manager to manage events across the enterprise – OEMCTL.

The OEMCTL Utility

The next monitoring utility that will be explained is used as part of Oracle Enterprise Manager (OEM) to provide many shared services for managing databases. OEM is the database management solution provided by Oracle Corporation. The OEMCTL utility manages the Oracle Management Server (OMS) used by OEM.

The OMS manages back-end application logic and stores information in the OEM repository. The functionality provided by the management server includes events, jobs, data sharing, and reports. The OMS serves as the middle tier between the management pack GUIs and the databases being managed. Multiple OMSs can exist in order to evenly distribute heavy workloads across this middle tier, although only one OMS can exist per node.

The repository used by OMS is simply a set of tables in a particular instance that support the management pack (Change, Diagnostics, Tuning) components of OEM.

Many commands are available from the *oemctl* executable at the OS level that help the DBA to manage the OMS. The following command will start the OMS:

```
oemctl start oms
```

If already running, the feedback from the command will respond, "The requested service has already been started."

The OMS is a Java application and when started, the Java Runtime (JRE) will be loaded into memory and consume approximately 40MB of RAM.

The method used to see if an OMS server is up and running is similar to the method in which a network administrator would check for TCP/IP communication to a remote host – ping.

```
oemctl ping oms
```

The *ping* command reports "the management server is running". To get a more detailed status of the OMS, the status command can be executed. This command, along with the stop command, requires the OMS Administrator's username and password in order to work. Optionally, the host name of the machine containing the OMS process can be specified if not the local machine. The default OMS Administrator username is password is *sysman/oem_temp*.

```
oemctl status oms <EM Username>/<EM Password>[@<OMS-hostname>]
```

This command requires the OMS administrator username and password. If not supplied, a Java application window will pop up and prompt for the username and password, as shown in Figure 5.3 below. Therefore, it is critical that the machine that initiates the command supports Java, otherwise the command will hang. For instance, if an attempt is made to obtain the status of the OMS by telnetting from a Windows machine to a UNIX box, the command will hang because the Java GUI application is unable to load. Again, this only applies when not specifying the username and password on the command line.

Figure 5.3 – OMS Login Screen 4

The result of the *oemctl* status command is shown below. Note the additional information that status provides over the ping command.

```
The Oracle Management Server on host [moorepc] is functioning
properly.

 The server has been up for 0 00:02:45.406

  Target database session count: 0 (session sharing is off)
  Operations queued for processing: 1
  Number of OMS systems in domain: 1 (moorepc)
  Number of administrators logged in: 1
```

```
Repository session pool depth: 15
Repository session count: 7 in-use and 4 available, pool
                          efficiency: 35%
```

The status command provides more details for the OMS environment. These include:

- **Target database session count** – The number of database connections established under the Databases folder in the navigator component of OEM.

- **Operations queued for processing** – Indicates the number of operations that are waiting to be processed. The activities may include sending e-mail, deleting events, submitting jobs, etc.

- **Number of OMS systems in domain** – Displays the number of OMS servers running. Multiple OMS servers can be created for scalability in large environments.

- **Number of administrators logged in** – The number of OEM administrators logged in to the OMS.

- **Repository session pool depth** – The number of database sessions reserved for OMS to submit jobs and register events. The default is 15 sessions and can be increased when heavy activity occurs.

- **Repository session count** – The number of repository sessions currently in the pool.

The OMS requires 7 sessions on startup. A repository session is needed to access information in the OEM repository. A specific number of sessions are retained in a pool to keep OMS from re-opening and closing sessions – a resource consumer. This parameter is not modifiable.

Stopping the OMS is performed by the command below. The stop command also requires the username and password.

```
oemctl stop oms <EM Username>/<EM Password>
```

Now that the basic operations of the *oemctl* executable have been covered, the next step is to enhance the functionality provided by the OMS. The DBA will decide the events about which to be concerned and what should be done about them. This is done through OMS Event Handlers.

OMS Event Handlers

Event handlers listen for events and respond in ways specified by the OMS Administrator. The OMS is capable of responding in two ways:

- **Event Logging** – Logs events to log files.
- **Command Execution** – Executes operating system commands in response to an event.

A triggered event can utilize one or both of these components. Event logging applies to those events in which the DBA might not possess a “ready made” automated resolution. For instance, the administrator might want to be notified (logged) when the archive destination directory is 90 percent full even though there is nothing that can automatically be done about it. Likewise, the DBA utilizes command execution when addressing events that can be handled automatically. For instance, when a tablespace becomes 95 percent full, a script could be executed that would add a datafile providing the needed space for the tablespace.

The following steps must be performed to set up event handling.

1. Stop the OMS.

```
oemctl stop oms sysman/oem_temp
```

2. Enable the event handler.

```
oemctl enable eventhandler
```

   Optionally, the default event handler can be viewed by:

```
oemctl dump eventhandler
```

```
***Current Configuration ***

The event handler is enabled for the OMS repository.
The event handler is enabled for the following OMS':
moorepc

The event handler will not  respect blackouts
There are 1 global filter(s):
Filter Name: allnodes
This filter will forward a notification if the following condition is met:
node = *


There are 3 adapter(s)

Adapter name: commandexecutor
```

```
Enabled: true
There are 1 filter(s) for this adapter
Filter Name: allevents
This filter will forward a notification if the following condition is met:
node = *

The command executor's execution timeout is 40 sec
The command executor has the following templates(s).
For all matching templates, the corresponding command will be executed.
Template Name: allevents2
Template String: echo %eventname%
This template will be used if the following filter is satisfied:
Filter Name: allevents2
This filter will forward a notification if the following condition is met:
eventname = *


Adapter name: eventlogger
Enabled: true
There are 1 filter(s) for this adapter
Filter Name: allevents
This filter will forward a notification if the following condition is met:
eventname = *

The event logger has the following templates(s):
Template Name: allevents
Template String: EVENTNAME:%eventname%  NODE: %node%    TARGET: %targetname%
SE
VERITY: %severity%  TIMESTAMP:  %timestamp%
This template will be used if the following filter is satisfied:
Filter Name: allevents
This filter will forward a notification if the following condition is met:
eventname = *
If the filter condition is met, the message will be logged to file
C:\oracle9i/s
ysman/log/eventhandler.log

Adapter name: plsqlexecutor
Enabled: true
There are 0 filter(s) for this adapter
The PL/SQL executor has the following templates(s).
For all matching templates, the corresponding command will be executed.
```

3. Start the OMS.

```
oemctl start oms
```

Loading event handlers is as simple as stopping the OMS, enabling the event handler, and then restarting the OMS. The next section will discuss ways to modify the event handler to provide the functionality needed.

Modifying the Event Handler

Modifying the event handler requires exporting it, editing it, and then loading it back into the OMS via the import command. The export command simply specifies the name of the file in which to export the event handler. The export command below will populate the file *myhandler* with the contents of the event handler.

```
oemctl export eventhandler myhandler
```

The event handler can then be edited with any text editor. On Windows systems, notepad will work (Figure 5.4).

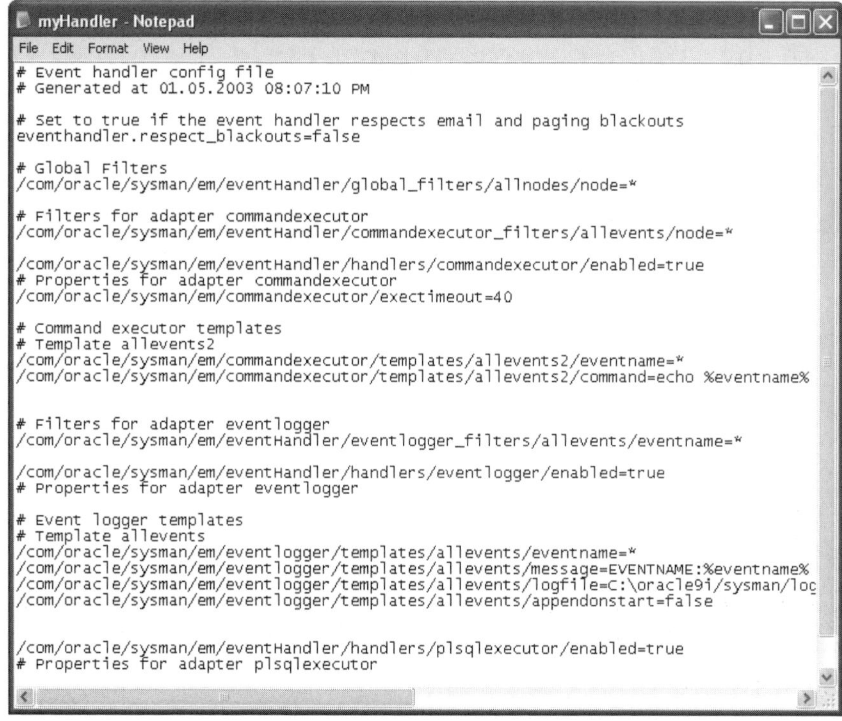

Figure 5.4 – Event Handler Editing with Notepad

The event handler file contains three main regions – blackouts, filters, and templates.

Blackouts are used to tell the OMS not to act on an event. For certain nodes, a DBA may not care about some events and they should not be handled. A setting of true tells the event handler not to process the event. A setting of false indicates that no blackout exists and the event should be processed.

Filters are used to determine which events are passed on to event logging or command execution. Each filter has a unique name. The default event handler above allows all events to be passed to both the command executor and event logger.

Templates specify exactly how to respond to the event. Templates for the event logger will determine how the data is formatted to the log. Templates specified for command execution include the actual OS command to execute for the event.

After any changes are made, the event handler needs to be imported back into the OMS:

```
oemctl import eventhandler myhandler
```

Now the OMS can be started again.

```
oemctl start OMS
```

To disable defined event handlers, execute the following command:

```
oemctl disable eventhandler
```

And finally, to view any errors encountered while using *oemctl*, view the log file in the *$ORACLE_HOME/sysman/log* directory.

Tuning the OMS

Manually tuning the OMS should rarely, if ever, be required. However, certain parameters are stored in the file *omsconfig.properties* located in the *$ORACLE_HOME/sysman/config* directory.

omsconfig.properties

```
#OMS Configuration Properties
#Mon Feb 04 14:38:27 CST 2002
OEM.REPOSITORY.PASSWORD=e642e7ff415[illegible]78c
oem.BootHost=localhost
OEM.EMCA_SHOW_WELCOME_PAGE=true
OEM.REPOSITORY.DATABASE=ORCL92
oem.BootPort=7771
OEM.REPOSITORY.USER=OMSUSER
OEM.REPOSITORY.DATABASE_ORIG=ORCL92

#The parameters below are used for tuning OMS
oms.vdg.max_out_conns=64
oms.vdg.max_in_conns=32
oms.repository.connect_timeout=120
oms.repository.connect_numTries=12
oms.vdp.ping_interval=2
oms.vdg.conn_retries=1
oms.vdg.conn_retries_delay=5
```

The parameters beginning with "OEM" are ones supplied by default in the properties file. These were set when the OMS database was created.

The parameters beginning with "oms" are not part of the default properties file. These are the parameters that are available to help the Administrator tune the OMS environment.

These include:

- ***oms.vdg.max_out_conns*** – The number of simultaneous outgoing connections supported by the OMS. If the number of servers managed by OMS is more than 64, set this parameter to that number. Otherwise, keep the default of 64.

- ***oms.vdg.max_in_conns*** – The number of simultaneous incoming transactions supported by the OMS. This should equal half the number of outgoing connections.

- ***oms.repository.connect_timeout*** – The number of seconds that the OMS will wait for a database that was shut down (the one holding the repository) to start back up again. This number should be set high enough to give the database ample time to start.

- ***oms.repository.connect_numTries*** – The number of tries that the OMS will make in order to connect to the repository database.

- ***oms.vdp.ping_interval*** – The number of minutes between OMS pings. The OMS pings each monitored server at the interval specified. If unable to ping a managed database, the OMS signals that the database is down. This ping interval should be set high enough to give the OMS enough time to ping all of the managed databases. If a low number is specified and a high number of databases are being monitored, many will be inaccurately flagged as down.

- ***oms.vdg.conn_retries*** – The number of times the OMS will attempt to re-ping one node in case the first ping failed.

- ***oms.vdg.conn_retries_delay*** – The amount of time between retries, and hence pings, of a managed database.

The *oemctl* utility provides options for the Administrator to manage the Oracle Management Server. The executable provides a mechanism to start, stop, ping, check the status, and even manage events. The OMS needs to be monitored and tuned just like any other software resource in order to maxmize its efficiency.

Application SQL is one of the most monitored elements of any database environment. The *dbms_xplan* utility provides an easy way for a DBA to view the optimizer execution path.

The *dbms_xplan* Utility

In version 9, Oracle finally provides a utility that formats the contents of the plan table. The plan table is one that is used to hold the results of an "Explain Plan" for a particular SQL statement. Explain Plan is used to generate and show the optimizer execution plan for a particular SQL statement.

The output from the explain plan shows the anticipated optimizer execution path, along with the estimated cost of the statement without actually executing the statement against the database.

The DBA or developer first needs to create the plan table. The DDL for this table is in the *$ORACLE_HOME/rdbms/admin/utllxplan.sql* file. The *create table* statement in the file is:

```
create table PLAN_TABLE (
        statement_id    varchar2(30),
        timestamp       date,
        remarks         varchar2(80),
        operation       varchar2(30),
        options         varchar2(255),
        object_node     varchar2(128),
        object_owner    varchar2(30),
        object_name     varchar2(30),
        object_instance numeric,
        object_type     varchar2(30),
        optimizer       varchar2(255),
        search_columns  number,
        id              numeric,
        parent_id       numeric,
        position        numeric,
        cost            numeric,
        cardinality     numeric,
        bytes           numeric,
        other_tag       varchar2(255),
        partition_start varchar2(255),
        partition_stop  varchar2(255),
        partition_id    numeric,
        other           long,
        distribution    varchar2(30),
        cpu_cost        numeric,
        io_cost         numeric,
        temp_space      numeric,
        access_predicates varchar2(4000),
        filter_predicates varchar2(4000));
```

This DDL can be submitted in any users schema. The next step in using *dbms_xplan* is running Explain Plan for a statement.

```
explain plan for
select * from employee where emp_id = 64523;
```

The command above will populate the plan table with the data returned from the optimizer. Next, the *dbms_xplan* utility can be used to view the output.

```
SQL> select * from table(dbms_xplan.display);

PLAN_TABLE_OUTPUT
---------------------------------------------------------------------------

---------------------------------------------------------------------------
| Id  | Operation                    |  Name        | Rows  | Bytes | Cost  |
---------------------------------------------------------------------------
|   0 | SELECT STATEMENT             |              |     1 |    24 |     2 |
|   1 |  TABLE ACCESS BY INDEX ROWID| EMPLOYEE     |     1 |    24 |     2 |
|*  2 |   INDEX RANGE SCAN           | EMP_IDX1     |     1 |       |     1 |
---------------------------------------------------------------------------

Predicate Information (identified by operation id):
---------------------------------------------------

PLAN_TABLE_OUTPUT
---------------------------------------------------------------------------

   2 - access("EMPLOYEE"."EMP_ID"=64523)

Note: cpu costing is off

15 rows selected.
```

The output above shows the query execution plan complete with formatting. This is the starting point for all expert SQL tuners.

dbms_xplan Options

dbms_xplan has only one procedure – *display*.

```
dbms_xplan.display (
     table_name   in   varchar2 default 'PLAN_TABLE',
     statement_id in   varchar2 default null,
     format       in   varchar2 default 'TYPICAL');
```

- ***table_name*** – The name of the plan table. If the plan table was named something other than the default (*plan_table*), then it needs to be specified here.

- ***statement_id*** – Displays only the plan table data for a particular statement id. When executing an Explain Plan, the user has the option of setting a *statement_id*. Use this option when the data for many statements is stored in the plan table.

- ***format*** – Four options apply to the format parameter.

  - ***BASIC*** – Minimum information from the execution plan is displayed – object name and operation.

  - ***TYPICAL*** – The most useful information from the plan table is displayed – ID, operation, object name, rows, bytes, and cost.

  - ***ALL*** – Maximum level of output. Includes everything in the TYPICAL plus SQL statements generated for parallel execution (if applicable).

  - ***SERIAL*** – Like TYPICAL but without parallel information regardless of whether or not the plan executes in parallel.

For more information on interpreting execution plan output see "Oracle High-Performance SQL Tuning" by Oracle Press.

dbms_xplan provides a useful feature to DBAs and developers. Although most DBAs and developers have explain plan scripts that they've used in prior versions of Oracle, the ease of this package makes it much more efficient. In addition, the formatting of execution plans for partitions and parallel queries is a valuable feature. DBAs should grant public access (execute) to this package and encourage developers to use it. By putting more tools into the hands of those who write the SQL, the better the database will perform.

Turning from SQL tuning to physical file monitoring, the next section will discuss how to detect and repair block corruption utilizing the *dbv* utility.

The *dbv* Utility (Database Verify)

The Database Verify utility (*dbv*) provides a mechanism to validate the structure of Oracle data files at the operating system level. It should be used on a regular basis to inspect data files for signs of corruption.

Although it can be used against open data files, the primary purpose of *dbv* is to verify the integrity of cold datafiles that would be used for a backup. If used against online datafiles, intermittent errors can occur and the utility should be executed again against the same file to verify accuracy. The utility can only be used against datafiles and not against control files or archived redo logs.

dbv Command Line Options

- ***File*** – The name of the Oracle datafile to verify. The file must be specified with full path name and file name including extension (.dbf).

- ***Start*** – The block within the file to begin the verification. If none is specified, *dbv* will begin at the first block in the file. This parameter should be used when processing large files in which the entire file does not need scanning.

- ***End*** – The last block in the data file to verify. If none is specified, *dbv* will process to the end of the file. This parameter should be used when processing large files in which the entire file does not need scanning.

- ***Blocksize*** – The database block size of the file that needs verification. This must be set to the *v$datafile.db_block_size* value for the data file.

If the block size is not specified, it will default to 2K. If the block size for the datafile does not equal the block size specified, *dbv* will terminate and print an error message:

```
dbv-00103: Specified BLOCKSIZE (2048) differs from actual
(8192)
```

- ***Logfile*** – The name of the file to direct the *dbv* output. If none is specified, the output will be sent to the terminal. When scheduling a *dbv*-based shell script, it will be this file that needs to be checked for corruption errors.

- ***Feedback*** – A progress meter that displays a dot for *n* pages examined in the file (FEEDBACK=10000). Use this to provide a status indicator when *dbv* is executed against large files. This is needed to indicate that the *dbv* process is actively processing a file. This option is obviously not needed when executing *dbv* through a scheduled shell script.

- ***Parfile*** - A parameter file that can contain any of these options. The *parfile* should be created once and used with every *dbv* command.

- ***Segment_ID*** – A parameter that will scan a segment regardless of the number of files it spans. The format is *segment_id=tsn.segfile.segblock*

- ***Userid*** – Used only in combination with *segment_id* to specify the username/password for the database connection.

Executing *dbv* and Interpreting the Output

dbv can be executed by specifying the file name and block size of the datafile. All other parameters are optional.

```
dbv file=/usr/oracle/asg920xr/datafiles/ASG920xrsys.dbf
   blocksize=8192
```

Once executed, *dbv* provides the following output for each file it verifies:

```
Total Pages Examined         : 52480
Total Pages Processed (Data) : 36617
Total Pages Failing   (Data) : 0
Total Pages Processed (Index): 4430
Total Pages Failing   (Index): 0
Total Pages Processed (Other): 1664
Total Pages Processed (Seg)  : 0
Total Pages Failing   (Seg)  : 0
Total Pages Empty            : 9769
Total Pages Marked Corrupt   : 0
Total Pages Influx           : 0
```

The output from *dbv* is not intuitive at first glance. Below are the definitions for each data item.

- **Total Pages Examined** – The number of blocks inspected by *dbv*. If the entire file was scanned, this value will match the BLOCKS column for the file in *v$datafile*.
- **Total Pages Processed (Data)** –The number of blocks inspected by *dbv* that contained table data.
- **Total Pages Failing (Data)** – The number of table blocks that have corruption.
- **Total Pages Processed (Index)** –The number of blocks inspected by *dbv* that contained index data.
- **Total Pages Failing (Index)** – The number of index blocks that are corrupted.

- **Total Pages Processed (Seg)** – This output is new to 9i and allows the command to specify a segment that spans multiple files.

- **Total Pages Failing (Seg)** – The number of segment data blocks that are corrupted.

- **Total Pages Empty** – Number of unused blocks discovered in the file.

- **Total Pages Marked Corrupt** – This is the most important one. It shows the number of corrupt blocks discovered during the scan.

- **Total Pages Influx** – The number of pages that were re-read due to the page being in use. This should only occur when executing *dbv* against hot datafiles and should never occur when running *dbv* against cold backup files.

Executing *dbv* against a Particular Segment

In order to execute *dbv* against a particular segment, the tablespace name, header file, and header block are needed. This command is useful when verifying particular objects that span multiple files. This is the only case, however, in which *dbv* requires a database connection.

```
SQL> select t.ts#, s.header_file, s.header_block
  2   from v$tablespace t, dba_segments s
  3   where s.owner = 'SCOTT'
  4   and s.segment_name='DEPARTMENT'
  5   and t.name = s.tablespace_name;


       TS# HEADER_FILE HEADER_BLOCK
---------- ----------- ------------
        15          12            9
```

Once these three data items are retrieved, the *dbv* command can be applied to a particular segment:

```
dbv userid=scott/tiger segment_id=15.12.9

Total Pages Examined         : 4
Total Pages Processed (Data) : 3
Total Pages Failing   (Data) : 0
Total Pages Processed (Index): 0
Total Pages Failing   (Index): 0
Total Pages Processed (Other): 0
Total Pages Processed (Seg)   : 1
Total Pages Failing   (Seg)  : 0
Total Pages Empty            : 0
Total Pages Marked Corrupt   : 0
Total Pages Influx           : 0
```

Automating *dbv*

DBAs should automate and execute the *dbv* utility on a regular basis. The following shell script (*dbv.ksh*) prompts for Oracle environment information, connects to the database, and produces a command file that can be executed at the convenience of the DBA. In this script, *dbv* is executed immediately after it's generated.

dbv.ksh

```
#!/bin/ksh
# Oracle Utilities
# dbv automation script
#
#
. oraenv
   wlogfile=dbv.${ORACLE_SID}
```

```
     SQLPLUS=${ORACLE_HOME}/bin/sqlplus
     $SQLPLUS -s  system/manager >> $wlogfile <<EOF
        set echo off feedback off verify off pages 0 termout off
            linesize 150
        spool dbv.cmd
        select 'dbv file=' || name || ' blocksize=' || block_size ||
          ' feedback=' || round(blocks*.10,0) -- 10 dots per file
          from v\$datafile;
        spool off
        set feedback on verify on pages24 echo on termout on
EOF
ksh dbv.cmd
#
# End of script
```

The *dbv*.ksh script formats a *dbv* command that can be executed from the UNIX command line. The logfile for the script is *dbv. ${ORACLE_SID}*. The results of the SQL statement are placed in the *dbv.cmd* file and this file is executed at the end of the script. Notice that a feedback was specified equivalent to one dot per each 10 percent of the file processed, in order to provide a status of *dbv*.

The contents of the *dbv.cmd* file are:

```
$ cat dbv.cmd

dbv file=/usr/oracle/asg920xr/datafiles/ASG920xrsys.dbf blocksize=8192 feedback=3200
dbv file=/usr/oracle/asg920xr/datafiles/undo.dbf blocksize=8192 feedback=1088
dbv file=/usr/oracle/asg920xr/datafiles/ASG920xray.dbf blocksize=8192 feedback=3200
dbv file=/usr/oracle/asg920xr/datafiles/aaa/UNDO1.dbf blocksize=8192 feedback=124
dbv file=/usr/oracle/asg920xr/datafiles/bbb/UNDO2.dbf blocksize=8192 feedback=26
dbv file=/usr/oracle/asg920xr/datafiles/ccc/UNDO3.dbf blocksize=8192 feedback=38
dbv file=/usr/oracle/asg920xr/datafiles/ddd/UNDO4.dbf blocksize=8192 feedback=51
dbv file=/usr/oracle/asg920xr/datafiles/aaa/UNDO5.dbf blocksize=8192 feedback=64
dbv file=/usr/oracle/asg920xr/datafiles/zzz/UNDO6.dbf blocksize=8192 feedback=13
dbv file=/usr/oracle/asg920xr/datafiles/aaa/undo_all1.dbf blocksize=8192 feedback=576
dbv file=/usr/oracle/asg920xr/datafiles/bbb/undo_all2.dbf blocksize=8192 feedback=26
dbv file=/usr/oracle/asg920xr/datafiles/ccc/undo_all3.dbf blocksize=8192 feedback=499
dbv file=/usr/oracle/asg920xr/datafiles/ddd/undo_all4.dbf blocksize=8192 feedback=602
dbv file=/usr/oracle/asg920xr/datafiles/aaa/undo_all5.dbf blocksize=8192 feedback=614
dbv file=/usr/oracle/asg920xr/datafiles/zzz/undo_all6.dbf blocksize=8192 feedback=13
dbv file=/data1/dbxray/datafiles/undo_all7.dbf blocksize=8192 feedback=602
dbv file=/data1/dbxray /datafiles/undo_tablespace_long2.dbf blocksize=8192 feedback=166
dbv file=/usr/oracle/asg920xr/datafiles/symbolic/UNDO8.dbf blocksize=8192 feedback=13
dbv file=/usr/oracle/asg920xr/datafiles/zzz/UNDO6a.dbf blocksize=8192feedback=1
dbv file=/usr/oracle/asg920xr/datafiles/davetest.dbf blocksize=8192 feedback=26
$
```

Notice in the *dbv.cmd* file above that the *block_size* is included for each datafile. In Oracle versions

8.1.7 and below, the following command would indicate the block size since it had to be consistent across the database.

```
SQL> show parameter db_block_size

NAME                                 TYPE        VALUE
------------------------------------ ----------- -------
db_block_size                        integer     8192
```

In version 9, each tablespace can have it's own block size and therefore it must be included at the datafile level.

The result of the execution of the *dbv.cmd* file is:

```
dbvERIFY: Release 9.2.0.1.0 - Production on Sun Dec 29 19:15:55 2002

Copyright (c) 1982, 2002, Oracle Corporation.  All rights reserved.

dbvERIFY - Verification starting : FILE = /usr/oracle/asg920xr/datafiles/ASG920xrsys.dbf
..........

dbvERIFY - Verification complete

Total Pages Examined         : 32000
Total Pages Processed (Data) : 16164
Total Pages Failing   (Data) : 0
Total Pages Processed (Index): 2520
Total Pages Failing   (Index): 0
Total Pages Processed (Other): 1230
Total Pages Processed (Seg)  : 0
Total Pages Failing   (Seg)  : 0
Total Pages Empty            : 12086
Total Pages Marked Corrupt   : 0
Total Pages Influx           : 0

dbvERIFY: Release 9.2.0.1.0 - Production on Sun Dec 29 19:16:06 2002

Copyright (c) 1982, 2002, Oracle Corporation.  All rights reserved.

dbvERIFY - Verification starting : FILE = /usr/oracle/asg920xr/datafiles/undo.dbf
..........

dbvERIFY - Verification complete
```

Notice the 10 dots displayed for each datafile as it was processed. Everything looks good in this output; no pages are marked as corrupt.

Alternative Block Checking Mechanisms

analyze table ... validate structure – The analyze command can do things that *dbv* cannot and vice-versa. The *analyze* command can validate that tables and indexes are in sync with each other. However, the analyze command only processes an object up to the point of its high water mark (HWM), whereas *dbv* processes all blocks in a file. Block corruption can occur in blocks above the HWM.

The *analyze* command would have to be executed against an open database for each object in the database. *dbv* can work against offline files and is much faster since it is strictly at the file level. In addition, the *analyze table* command places an exclusive lock on the object being analyzed. Alternatively, *dbv* works outside of the database in "read only" mode against the datafiles and does not lock anything. Any errors encountered by the *analyze table* command are reported in the session trace file in the user dump destination directory.

db_block_checking=true – The default is false for this configuration parameter which is system modifiable:

```
ALTER SYSTEM SET DB_BLOCK_CHECKING = TRUE;
```

When true, Oracle performs block checks for all data blocks making sure that all data in the block is consistent.

Block checking provides early detection of block corruption, however, it costs between 1-10% in overhead on the database. The more block writes that occur on a system (INSERT, UPDATE, DELETE), the more costly it becomes. Any errors encountered by block checking result in an ORA-600 level message. Before setting this parameter to TRUE, first execute *dbv* against the datafiles to make sure they are free of corruption. Even when FALSE, Oracle still provides block checking for the *system* tablespace.

Handling Corruption

Some errors reported by *dbv* are transient in nature. Therefore, the utility should be executed on the suspect file again to confirm block corruption. If problems are again reported in the same page locations, then the file is indeed corrupt.

Once one or more corrupted blocks are detected, the DBA must resolve the issue. Below are some options available to the DBA to address block corruption:

- **Drop and re-create the corrupted object** – If the loss of data is not an issue, this is the preferred approach. For Data Warehouses, the data can be reloaded from external sources and the loss of data is minor. However, for OLTP tables (*customer_orders*), no data can be lost without a serious negative impact on the business.

If the object is an index, rebuild it. If a few blocks are corrupt, determine which object(s) are causing the corruption. This can be done in the query below by mapping the physical file location to an object(s) contained in the file.

```
select tablespace_name, segment_type, owner,
       segment_name
 from dba_extents
 where file_id = <corrupted file id>
 and <Block #>  between block_id AND block_id + blocks-1;
```

- **Restore the file from a backup** – The tried and true method for restoring good blocks back into the datafiles.

- **Use *dbms_repair*** – Dealing with block corruption is always a risky proposition so limit the use of *dbms_repair* to extreme situations. *dbms_repair* is a package supplied by Oracle that identifies and repairs block corruption (described in next section).

If the first two options are unacceptable, using *dbms_repair* can resolve some block corruption issues.

dbv is a useful utility to inspect datafiles for block corruption. It should be used primarily against offline datafiles on a regular basis. In should be used in combination with other corruption detection mechanisms, including the analyze table command and *init.ora* parameters.

For online checking, the configuration parameter *db_block_checking* should be enabled, provided the overhead incurred on the database is at an acceptable level. Finally, when corrupted blocks are detected, the DBA should choose the most appropriate method of recovery – be it a restore, a rebuild of the object, or utilizing the *dbms_repair* utility.

The *dbms_repair* Utility

dbms_repair is a utility that can detect and repair block corruption within Oracle. It is provided by Oracle as part of the standard database installation.

Configuring the Environment

Two tables must first be created under the SYS schema before the *dbms_repair* utility can be used. Fortunately, a procedure in the package itself (*admin_tables*) creates these tables and eliminates the need to hunt for a script in *$ORACLE_HOME/rdbms/admin*.

```
dbms_repair.ADMIN_TABLES (
   table_name  IN   VARCHAR2,
   table_type  IN   BINARY_INTEGER,
   action      IN   BINARY_INTEGER,
   tablespace  IN   VARCHAR2         DEFAULT NULL);
```

- ***table_name*** – The name of the table to be processed, as determined by the action.
- ***table_type*** – Either *orphan_table* or *repair_table*.

- ***action*** – Either *create_action*, *purge_action* or *drop_action*. When *create_action* is specified, the table will be created in the SYS schema. *purge_action* deletes all rows in the table that apply to objects that no longer exist. *drop_action* will drop the table.

- ***tablespace*** – The tablespace in which the newly created table will reside. This tablespace must already exist.

The following command will be used to create the two tables needed. The command will be executed twice with different parameters, once for the *repair* table and once for the *orphan* table.

```
begin
  dbms_repair.admin_tables(
     table_name => 'REPAIR_TEST',
     table_type => dbms_repair.repair_table,
     action     => dbms_repair.create_action,
     tablespace => 'SCOTTWORK'
   );
end;

begin
  dbms_repair.admin_tables(
     table_name => 'ORPHAN_TEST',
     table_type => dbms_repair.orphan_table,
     action     => dbms_repair.create_action,
     tablespace => 'SCOTTWORK'
   );
end;
```

The two tables are now created. A describe of the two tables reveals the following:

```
SQL> desc repair_test;

 Name                                      Null?    Type
 ----------------------------------------- -------- ----------------
 OBJECT_ID                                 NOT NULL NUMBER
 TABLESPACE_ID                             NOT NULL NUMBER
 RELATIVE_FILE_ID                          NOT NULL NUMBER
 BLOCK_ID                                  NOT NULL NUMBER
 CORRUPT_TYPE                              NOT NULL NUMBER
 SCHEMA_NAME                               NOT NULL VARCHAR2(30)
 OBJECT_NAME                               NOT NULL VARCHAR2(30)
 BASEOBJECT_NAME                                    VARCHAR2(30)
 PARTITION_NAME                                     VARCHAR2(30)
 CORRUPT_DESCRIPTION                                VARCHAR2(2000)
 REPAIR_DESCRIPTION                                 VARCHAR2(200)
 MARKED_CORRUPT                            NOT NULL VARCHAR2(10)
 CHECK_TIMESTAMP                           NOT NULL DATE
 FIX_TIMESTAMP                                      DATE
 REFORMAT_TIMESTAMP                                 DATE

SQL> desc orphan_test

 Name                                      Null?    Type
 ----------------------------------------- -------- ----------------
 SCHEMA_NAME                               NOT NULL VARCHAR2(30)
 INDEX_NAME                                NOT NULL VARCHAR2(30)
 IPART_NAME                                         VARCHAR2(30)
 INDEX_ID                                  NOT NULL NUMBER
 TABLE_NAME                                NOT NULL VARCHAR2(30)
 PART_NAME                                          VARCHAR2(30)
 TABLE_ID                                  NOT NULL NUMBER
 KEYROWID                                  NOT NULL ROWID
 KEY                                       NOT NULL ROWID
 DUMP_TIMESTAMP                            NOT NULL DATE
```

Repair tables will contain those objects that have corrupted blocks. Orphan tables, on the other hand, are used to contain indexes that point to corrupted data

Finding Corrupt Blocks

The *dbms_repair* utility provides a mechanism to search for corrupt database blocks. Below is the syntax for the *check_objects* procedure. Note that the only OUT parameter is the *corrupt_count.*

```
dbms_repair.CHECK_OBJECT (
   schema_name        IN  VARCHAR2,
   object_name        IN  VARCHAR2,
   partition_name     IN  VARCHAR2        DEFAULT NULL,
   object_type        IN  BINARY_INTEGER DEFAULT TABLE_OBJECT,
   repair_table_name  IN  VARCHAR2        DEFAULT 'REPAIR_TABLE',
   flags              IN  BINARY_INTEGER DEFAULT NULL,
   relative_fno       IN  BINARY_INTEGER DEFAULT NULL,
   block_start        IN  BINARY_INTEGER DEFAULT NULL,
   block_end          IN  BINARY_INTEGER DEFAULT NULL,
   corrupt_count      OUT BINARY_INTEGER);
```

- ***schema_name*** – Schema name of the object to be checked for corruption.

- ***object_name*** – Name of the table or index that will be checked for corruption.

- ***partition_name*** – Partition or sub-partition name to be checked.

- ***object_type*** – Either *TABLE_OBJECT* or *INDEX_OBJECT* as specified as an enumeration (*dbms_repair.table_object*).

- ***repair_table_name*** – The name of the repair table to be populated in the SYS schema.

- ***flags*** – Not used.

- ***relative_fno*** – The relative file number to be used when specifying a block range to be checked.

- ***block_start*** – The first block in the block range to begin checking.

- ***block_end*** – The last block in the block range to check.

- ***corrupt_count*** – The number of corrupt blocks discovered.

The code below will check the *scott.employee* table for corruption and report the number of corrupted blocks.

dbms_repair.sql

```
set serveroutput on
declare corr_count binary_integer;
begin
corr_count := 0;
dbms_repair.CHECK_OBJECT (
   schema_name       => 'SCOTT',
   object_name       => 'EMPLOYEE',
   partition_name    => null,
   object_type       => dbms_repair.table_object,
   repair_table_name => 'REPAIR_TEST',
   flags             => null,
   relative_fno      => null,
   block_start       => null,
   block_end         => null,
   corrupt_count     => corr_count
   );
dbms_output.put_line(to_char(corr_count));
end;
/

# Corrupt Blocks =0

PL/SQL procedure successfully completed.
```

Once executed, the table *repair_test* can be queried in order to find more about corrupt blocks. In this case, no rows exist in the table. The repair table is only populated if the *check_object* procedure did indeed find corrupt blocks, so no rows in this table is good news!

Repairing Corrupt Blocks

The *dbms_repair* utility provides a mechanism to repair the corrupt database blocks, the *fix_corrupt_blocks* procedure. Corrupt blocks are not really repaired, but instead are simply marked as corrupt.

Below is the syntax for the *fix_corrupt_blocks* procedure. Note that the only OUT parameter is the *fix_count.*

```
dbms_repair.FIX_CORRUPT_BLOCKS (
   schema_name        IN  VARCHAR2,
   object_name        IN  VARCHAR2,
   partition_name     IN  VARCHAR2        DEFAULT NULL,
   object_type        IN  BINARY_INTEGER DEFAULT TABLE_OBJECT,
   repair_table_name IN  VARCHAR2        DEFAULT 'REPAIR_TABLE',
   flags              IN  BINARY_INTEGER DEFAULT NULL,
   fix_count          OUT BINARY_INTEGER);
```

- ***schema_name*** - The name of the schema containing the object with corrupt blocks.

- ***object_name*** – The name of the object needing repair.

- ***partition_name*** – The name of the partition or subpartition to process. If none is specified and the object is partitioned, all partitions will be processed.

- ***object_type*** - Either *table_object* or *index_object* as specified as an enumeration.

- ***repair_table_name*** – The name of the repair table.

- ***flags*** – Not used.

- ***fix_count*** – The number of blocks fixed. This should equal the same number of corrupt blocks reported.

If the object repaired is a table, then any corresponding index also needs to be fixed. The *dump_orphan_keys* procedure will indicate if any keys are broken. If they are, the index will need to be rebuilt.

Rebuilding Freelists

The *dbms_repair* utility provides a mechanism to rebuild the impacted freelists and bitmap entries after fixing block corruption. This procedure recreates the header portion of the datafile, allowing Oracle to use the newly repaired blocks.

Below is the syntax for the *rebuild_freelists* procedure:

```
dbms_repair.REBUILD_FREELISTS (
   schema_name    IN VARCHAR2,
   partition_name IN VARCHAR2       DEFAULT NULL,
   object_type    IN BINARY_INTEGER DEFAULT TABLE_OBJECT);
```

- ***schema_name*** – The name of the schema containing the object whose freelists need rebuilding.

- ***partition_name*** – The name of the partition or subpartition whose freelists are to be rebuilt.

- ***object_type*** – Either *TABLE_OBJECT* or *INDEX_OBJECT* as specified as an enumeration.

dbms_repair provides a new method of addressing ORA-600 errors dealing with block corruption. The utility is very easy to use and very functional. As described earlier, it is one of many potential solutions when resolving block corruption. *dbms_repair* does basically the same thing as *analyze table ... validate structure.*

Summary

This chapter has discussed many useful utilities that can be used to monitor and tune Oracle database performance. *dbms_alert* can be used for asynchronous communication from the database to any other machine. It is up to the user of *dbms_alert* to define the types of events they are interested. *utl_smtp* can be used to send e-mails from the database to any valid e-mail address. *oemctl* takes alerting to a higher level by supervising the Oracle Management Server, which provides monitoring and issues alerts on events across an entire environment.

When tuning SQL statements, *dbms_xplan* provides formatting capability on the contents of the plan table. This package should be used to generate anticipated optimizer statistics without actually executing the query.

When monitoring the database for corrupted blocks, *dbv* should be used to check the integrity of the datafiles. When corruption is detected, many options are available to the DBA, including using the *dbms_repair* utility.

The next chapter will discuss utilities that are used for tracing and debugging database issues.

Chapter 6

Tracing Utilities

This chapter will discuss those utilities that aid a DBA in tracing database activity. Tracing is an activity that is critical to a DBA in order to accurately detect and diagnose all sorts of database issues. The utilities covered in this chapter include *tkprof*, *autotrace*, Oracle Trace, *oradebug* and Trace Analyzer.

The first utility described in this chapter is one of the most underutilized utilities within Oracle – *tkprof*.

Formatting Trace Files with *tkprof*

tkprof is one of the most useful utilities available to DBAs for diagnosing performance issues. It essentially formats a trace file into a more readable format for performance analysis. The DBA can then identify and resolve performance issues such as poor SQL, indexing, and wait events.

tkprof has been historically difficult to use for many reasons. First, the entire process of enabling tracing, finding trace files, and executing the utility against them is a burdensome task. Once the DBA finally has the trace file output, the typical response is "Now what do I do"? Second, even though *tkprof* formats the data, it lacks any additional insight needed to remedy the problems revealed. In fact, problems are not even highlighted, thereby putting more work on the DBA to analyze the output, assess the problems, and determine what to do.

Why, When *tkprof*?

The DBA will use *tkprof* and session tracing when the database or a particular session is having performance problems. *tkprof* will generally be used infrequently when researching a very particular performance issue. A user may complain that the response time for a session is abysmal compared to the prior week. Session tracing and *tkprof* can be used to see exactly what is happening on the database, thus enabling the DBA to take corrective action.

The utility can also be used to view SQL that is being executed for an application. In some situations, this will be the only mechanism a DBA will have to view SQL. These situations include the execution of encrypted PL/SQL code on the database or submission of SQL statements from third party applications.

Analyzing *tkprof* Results

So what should DBAs be looking for? Here's a small checklist of items to watch for in *tkprof* formatted files:

- **Compare the number of parses to number of executions.** A well-tuned system will have one parse per *n* executions of a statement and will eliminate the re-parsing of the same statement.

- **Search for SQL statements that do not use bind variables (:variable).** These statements should be modified to use bind variables.

- **Identify those statements that perform full table scans, multiple disk reads, and high CPU consumption.** These performance benchmarks are defined by the DBA and need to be tailored to each database. What may be considered a high number of disk reads for an OLTP application may not even be minimal for a data warehouse implementation.

The *tkprof* process will be explained in six easy steps.

Step 1: Check the Environment

Before tracing can be enabled, the environment must first be configured by performing the following steps:

- **Enable Timed Statistics** – This parameter enables the collection of certain vital statistics such as CPU execution time, wait events, and elapsed times. The resulting trace output is more meaningful with these statistics. The command to enable timed statistics is:

```
ALTER SYSTEM SET TIMED_STATISTICS = TRUE;
```

- **Check the User Dump Destination Directory** – The trace files generated by Oracle can be numerous and large. These files are placed by Oracle in the *user_dump_dest* directory as specified in the *init.ora.* The user dump destination can also be specified for a single session using the *alter session* command. Make sure that enough space exists on the device to support the number of trace files that you expect to generate.

```
SQL> select value
        from v$parameter
        where name = 'user_dump_dest';

VALUE
---------------------------------
C:\oracle9i\admin\ORCL92\udump
```

Once the directory name is obtained, the corresponding space command (OS dependent) will report the amount of available space. Delete unwanted trace files before starting a new trace to free up the disk space.

Step 2: Turn Tracing On

The next step in the process is to enable tracing. By default, tracing is disabled due to the burden (5-10%) it places on the database. Tracing can be defined at the session level:

```
ALTER SESSION SET SQL_TRACE = TRUE;

DBMS_SESSION.SET_SQL_TRACE(TRUE);
```

A DBA may enable tracing for another user's session by using the following statement:

```
DBMS_SYSTEM.SET_SQL_TRACE_IN_SESSION(sid,serial#,true);
```

The *sid* (Session ID) and serial# can be obtained from the *v$session* view. This package is owned by the SYS user and therefore the executor must be SYS or be granted the EXECUTE privilege by SYS user.

Once tracing is enabled, Oracle generates and stores the statistics in the trace file. The trace file name is version specific. Table 5.1 below contains the version naming conventions for foreground processes.

Version	**Naming Convention**	**Example**
7.3.4	snnn_pid.trc	s000_4714.trc
8.0.5	ora_pid_trc	ora_2345.trc
8.1.7	ora_pid_instance.trc	ora_13737_asgard81.trc
9.x	instance_ora_pid.trc	asgard91_ora_15313.trc

Table 5.1 - Oracle Trace File Naming Conventions

Supplied with this information, the DBA can construct a query that will return the trace file for a given session or for all sessions attached to the database. The query below (*Users_Trace_Files.sql*) will show the trace file name for each process.

users_trace_files.sql

```
column username format a10
column trace_file format a70
select b.username, c.value || '\' || lower(d.value) || '_ora_' ||
       to_char(a.spid, 'fm00000') || '.trc' "TRACE_FILE"
from v$process a, v$session b, v$parameter c, v$parameter d
where a.addr    = b.paddr
and c.name      = 'user_dump_dest'
and d.name      = 'db_name'
and b.username is not null;

USERNAME   TRACE_FILE
---------- ----------------------------------------------------------
SYS        C:\oracle9i\admin\ORCL92\udump\ORCL92_ora_03164.trc
SCOTT      C:\oracle9i\admin\ORCL92\udump\ORCL92_ora_02264.trc
DAVE       C:\oracle9i\admin\ORCL92\udump\ORCL92_ora_03578.trc
```

Notice that the trace files are for each session and not for each named user. Given that the SYS user has two connections to the database, the commands for each session would be in separate trace files.

The query can be modified to return the file name for the currently connected session. *My_trace_file.sql* will return the file name for the current session.

my_trace_file.sql

```
select c.value || '\' || lower(d.value) || '_ora_' ||
       to_char(a.spid, 'fm00000') || '.trc' "TRACE FILE"
from v$process a, v$session b, v$parameter c, v$parameter d
where a.addr = b.paddr
and b.audsid = userenv('sessionid')
and c.name   = 'user_dump_dest'
and d.name   = 'db_name';

TRACE FILE
---------------------------------------------------------------
C:\oracle9i\admin\ORCL92\udump\ORCL92_ora_03164.trc
```

Both queries above generate the trace file names (with Oracle9i on Windows XP) that would exist if the session were to be traced. However, there is no indication in any *v$* view that a session is currently being traced. The only way to really know if tracing is being performed is to inspect the file names and dates in *user_dump_dest* directory. For this reason, a DBA should not trace a session indefinitely, as it will continue to consume both performance resources and file system resources. If the *user_dump_dest* directory fills, the Oracle database will come to a screeching halt.

When the DBA determines that enough data has been gathered, the next step is to disable tracing.

Step 3: Turn Tracing Off

The same options that we use to enable tracing are used to disable it. These include:

```
ALTER SESSION SET SQL_TRACE = FALSE;

DBMS_SESSION.SET_SQL_TRACE(FALSE);
```

To disable tracing for another user's session use:

```
DBMS_SYSTEM.SET_SQL_TRACE_IN_SESSION(sid,serial#,false);
```

This process is a perfect candidate for automation. The code below (*start_trace.sql*) creates a stored procedure that automates all the steps discussed so far. It can also serve as a wrapper for the standard methods of enabling tracing. *Start_trace.sql* accepts the *sid* and *serial#* for the session that needs tracing. It requires that a time interval, in seconds, be set to run the trace so that it doesn't run perpetually and bog down the session. When the time has elapsed, it will disable tracing for the session and send the relevant trace information: user, time, and trace file name.

start_trace.sql

```
create or replace procedure start_trace
 (
   v_sid     in number,
   v_serial# in number,
   seconds   in number)


---------------------------------------------
-- 2003 - Oracle Utilities
-- D. Moore
--
-- This procedure serves as a wrapper to
-- session tracing.  It accepts
-- a sid and serial#, along with the amount of
-- time in seconds that the trace should last.
-- The trace will be stopped when that time
-- period expires.  After tracing is turned
-- off, the name of the trace file will be
-- displayed.
---------------------------------------------


IS
   v_user           varchar2 (32);
   stop_trace_cmd   varchar2 (200);
   duration         number;
   v_spid           number;
   dump_dest        varchar2 (200);
   db_name          varchar2 (32);
   v_version        varchar2 (32);
   v_compatible     varchar2 (32);
   file_name        varchar2 (32);
   no_session_found exception;

BEGIN
    begin
      select a.username, b.spid into v_user,v_spid
         from v$session a, v$process b
         where a.sid     = v_sid  and
               a.serial# = v_serial# and
               a.paddr   = b.addr;
      exception
      when NO_DATA_FOUND then
```

```
    raise no_session_found;

end;

dbms_system.set_sql_trace_in_session(v_sid,v_serial#,true);
dbms_output.put_line('Tracing Started for User: '
            || v_user);
dbms_output.put_line('Tracing Start Time: '
            || TO_CHAR(SYSDATE, 'MM-DD-YYYY HH24:MI:SS'));


--------------------------------------------------
-- Sleep for the amount of seconds specified as
-- seconds input parameter.  When complete, stop
-- the tracing and display the resulting trace file
-- name
--------------------------------------------------

if seconds is null then
   duration := 60;
else
   duration := seconds;
end if;

dbms_lock.sleep(duration);

-- the time alotted has now expired. Disable
-- tracing and output the trace file information

dbms_system.set_sql_trace_in_session(v_sid,v_serial#,false);
dbms_output.put_line ('Tracing Stop Time: '
            || TO_CHAR(SYSDATE, 'MM-DD-YYYY HH24:MI:SS'));

-- get all of the data needed to format the trace file name

select value into dump_dest
   from v$parameter
   where name = 'user_dump_dest';

select value into db_name
   from v$parameter
   where name = 'db_name';

-- we need the version of the database in order to determine
-- the naming scheme for the trace file

dbms_utility.db_version(v_version, v_compatible);

if substr(v_version,1,1) = '9' then
   file_name := db_name || '_ora_' || v_spid || '.trc';
elsif substr(v_version,1,3) = '8.1' then
   file_name := 'ora_' || v_spid || '_' || db_name || '.trc';
elsif substr(v_version,1,3) = '8.0' then
   file_name := 'ora_' || v_spid || '.trc';
end if;

dbms_output.put_line('Trace Directory: ' || dump_dest);
dbms_output.put_line('Trace Filename: ' || file_name);
```

```
    exception
      when no_session_found then
         dbms_output.put_line('No session found for sid and serial#
                                    specified');

END start_trace;
```

The output from *start_trace.sql* is displayed below. The time interval specified was 30 and we can see the elapsed time of the trace in the timestamps below.

```
SQL> exec start_trace(17, 6157, 30);

Tracing Started for User: SCOTT
Tracing Start Time: 12-26-2002 14:55:12
Tracing Stop Time: 12-26-2002 14:55:42
Trace Directory: C:\oracle9i\admin\ORCL92\udump
Trace Filename: ORCL92_ora_5472.trc
```

The next step is to run *tkprof* against the trace file.

Step 4: Locate Trace File and Execute *tkprof*

Locating the file is easy because the script above gives us the file name. *tkprof* will format the raw trace file, although the file is somewhat readable without *tkprof*.

```
Raw Trace File


PARSING IN CURSOR #1 len=44 dep=0 uid=59 oct=3 lid=59 tim=535446373886 hv=159129
656 ad='12cbbe70'
 select * from employee where emp_id = 87933
END OF STMT
PARSE #1:c=0,e=37469,p=0,cr=0,cu=0,mis=1,r=0,dep=0,og=4,tim=535446373874
EXEC #1:c=0,e=71,p=0,cr=0,cu=0,mis=0,r=0,dep=0,og=4,tim=535446375834
FETCH #1:c=31250,e=42564,p=10,cr=416,cu=0,mis=0,r=1,dep=0,og=4,tim=535446418910
FETCH #1:c=0,e=3852,p=0,cr=57,cu=0,mis=0,r=0,dep=0,og=4,tim=535446424026
STAT #1 id=1 cnt=1 pid=0 pos=1 obj=30497 op='TABLE ACCESS FULL EMPLOYEE '
=====================
PARSING IN CURSOR #1 len=44 dep=0 uid=59 oct=3 lid=59 tim=535448474894 hv=159129
656 ad='12cbbe70'
 select * from employee where emp_id = 87933
END OF STMT
PARSE #1:c=0,e=146,p=0,cr=0,cu=0,mis=0,r=0,dep=0,og=4,tim=535448474882
EXEC #1:c=0,e=76,p=0,cr=0,cu=0,mis=0,r=0,dep=0,og=4,tim=535448476767
FETCH #1:c=31250,e=30553,p=12,cr=416,cu=0,mis=0,r=1,dep=0,og=4,tim=535448507870
FETCH #1:c=15625,e=3832,p=0,cr=57,cu=0,mis=0,r=0,dep=0,og=4,tim=535448512927
STAT #1 id=1 cnt=1 pid=0 pos=1 obj=30497 op='TABLE ACCESS FULL EMPLOYEE '
=====================
PARSING IN CURSOR #1 len=44 dep=0 uid=59 oct=3 lid=59 tim=535449209407 hv=159129
656 ad='12cbbe70'
```

```
 select * from employee where emp_id = 87933
END OF STMT
PARSE #1:c=0,e=111,p=0,cr=0,cu=0,mis=0,r=0,dep=0,og=4,tim=535449209395
EXEC #1:c=0,e=74,p=0,cr=0,cu=0,mis=0,r=0,dep=0,og=4,tim=535449211302
FETCH #1:c=31250,e=32623,p=8,cr=416,cu=0,mis=0,r=1,dep=0,og=4,tim=535449244513
FETCH #1:c=15625,e=3918,p=0,cr=57,cu=0,mis=0,r=0,dep=0,og=4,tim=535449249648
STAT #1 id=1 cnt=1 pid=0 pos=1 obj=30497 op='TABLE ACCESS FULL EMPLOYEE '
=====================
PARSING IN CURSOR #1 len=44 dep=0 uid=59 oct=3 lid=59 tim=535449801444 hv=159129
656 ad='12cbbe70'
 select * from employee where emp_id = 87933
END OF STMT
PARSE #1:c=0,e=102,p=0,cr=0,cu=0,mis=0,r=0,dep=0,og=4,tim=535449801433
EXEC #1:c=0,e=74,p=0,cr=0,cu=0,mis=0,r=0,dep=0,og=4,tim=535449803310
FETCH #1:c=31250,e=31503,p=7,cr=416,cu=0,mis=0,r=1,dep=0,og=4,tim=535449835358
FETCH #1:c=15625,e=4039,p=0,cr=57,cu=0,mis=0,r=0,dep=0,og=4,tim=535449840721
STAT #1 id=1 cnt=1 pid=0 pos=1 obj=30497 op='TABLE ACCESS FULL EMPLOYEE '
=====================
PARSING IN CURSOR #1 len=44 dep=0 uid=59 oct=3 lid=59 tim=535450369301 hv=159129
656 ad='12cbbe70'
 select * from employee where emp_id = 87933
END OF STMT
PARSE #1:c=0,e=101,p=0,cr=0,cu=0,mis=0,r=0,dep=0,og=4,tim=535450369290
EXEC #1:c=0,e=76,p=0,cr=0,cu=0,mis=0,r=0,dep=0,og=4,tim=535450371203
FETCH #1:c=15625,e=28362,p=5,cr=416,cu=0,mis=0,r=1,dep=0,og=4,tim=535450400245
FETCH #1:c=15625,e=4333,p=0,cr=57,cu=0,mis=0,r=0,dep=0,og=4,tim=535450405578
STAT #1 id=1 cnt=1 pid=0 pos=1 obj=30497 op='TABLE ACCESS FULL EMPLOYEE '
=====================
```

With minimal effort, a programmer could create a trace file parser and formatter similar to *tkprof* that provides the trace data in a format even more suitable for analysis.

The *tkprof* command can now be executed from the operating system prompt.

```
C:\oracle9i\admin\ORCL92\udump>tkprof ORCL92_ora_3064.trc
output.txt insert=tkprof.sql record=Allsql.sql

tkprof: Release 9.2.0.1.0 - Production on Thu Dec 26 13:22:29 2002

Copyright (c) 1982, 2002, Oracle Corporation.  All rights reserved.
```

Based on the command above, *tkprof* will process the file *ORCL92_ora_3064.trc* and format the results in the file *output.txt.* Two other files were also created (*tkprof.sql*, *allsql.sql*) that will be discussed later.

Step 5: Analyze *tkprof* Output

This is the most difficult step in the process. Each *tkprof* output file contains a header, body, and summary section. The header simply displays the trace file name, definitions, and sort options selected. The body contains the performance metrics for SQL statements. The summary section contains an aggregate of performance statistics for all SQL statements in the file.

```
tkprof Output

tkprof: Release 9.2.0.1.0 - Production on Tue Dec 24 15:32:43 2002

Copyright (c) 1982, 2002, Oracle Corporation.  All rights reserved.

Trace file: ORCL92_ora_3064.trc
Sort options: default

********************************************************************************

count    = number of times OCI procedure was executed
cpu      = cpu time in seconds executing
elapsed  = elapsed time in seconds executing
disk     = number of physical reads of buffers from disk
query    = number of buffers gotten for consistent read
current  = number of buffers gotten in current mode (usually for update)
rows     = number of rows processed by the fetch or execute call
********************************************************************************


select *
from
 employee where emp_id = 87933

call     count       cpu    elapsed       disk      query    current        rows

------- ------  -------- ---------- ---------- ---------- ----------  ----------

Parse       10      0.00       0.03          0          0          0           0

Execute     10      0.00       0.00          0          0          0           0

Fetch       20      0.34       0.35         72       4730          0          10

------- ------  -------- ---------- ---------- ---------- ----------  ----------

total       40      0.34       0.39         72       4730          0          10

Misses in library cache during parse: 1
Optimizer goal: CHOOSE
Parsing user id: 59

Rows     Row Source Operation
-------  ---------------------------------------------------
      1  TABLE ACCESS FULL EMPLOYEE

********************************************************************************
```

The output displays a table of performance metrics after each unique SQL statement. Each row in the table corresponds to each of the three steps required in SQL processing.

1. **Parse** – The translation of the SQL into an execution plan. This step includes syntax checks, permissions, and all object dependencies.

2. **Execute** – The actual execution of the statement.

3. **Fetch** – The number of rows returned for a SELECT statement.

The table columns include the following:

- **Count** – The number of times a statement was parsed, executed, or fetched.

- **CPU** – The total CPU time in seconds for all parse, execute, or fetch calls.

- **Elapsed** – Total elapsed time in seconds for all parse, execute, or fetch calls.

- **Disk** – The number of physical disk reads from the datafiles for all parse, execute, or fetch calls.

- **Query** – The number of buffers retrieved for all parse, execute, or fetch calls.

- **Current** – The number of buffers retrieved in current mode (INSERT, UPDATE, or DELETE statements).

Observe from the *tkprof* output above that the SQL statement performed a *TABLE ACCESS FULL*, meaning a full-table scan. Full-table scans can degrade performance, especially when accessing a small subset of the data in a table. In this case, the query is selecting one row, yet all 100,000 rows in the table are scanned. This is a perfect situation to add an index on the *EMP_ID* column of the *EMPLOYEE* table:

```
SQL> CREATE INDEX emp_idx1 ON employee (emp_id);

Index created.
```

Let's examine the performance of this query again, this time with the index enabled.

```
select *
from
 employee where emp_id = 87933

call     count       cpu    elapsed       disk      query    current        rows
------- ------  -------- ---------- ---------- ---------- ----------  ----------

Parse        1      0.03       0.05          1          1          0           0

Execute      1      0.00       0.00          0          0          0           0

Fetch        2      0.00       0.03          3          4          0           1

------- ------  -------- ---------- ---------- ---------- ----------  ----------

total        4      0.03       0.09          4          5          0           1

Misses in library cache during parse: 1
Optimizer goal: CHOOSE
Parsing user id: 59

Rows     Row Source Operation
-------  ---------------------------------------------------
      1  TABLE ACCESS BY INDEX ROWID EMPLOYEE
      1   INDEX RANGE SCAN EMP_IDX1 (object id 30498)

********************************************************************************
```

The CPU speed improved by a multiple of 11 (.03 vs. .34) compared to the benchmark before the index was added.

Step 6: Load *tkprof* Results into Tables

Loading *tkprof* data into the database is optional, but it can be worthwhile for those DBAs who want historical data or the ability to access data via SQL queries to generate reports. The command used earlier specified *insert=tkprof.sql* which generated the following SQL in *tkprof.sql*:

```
CREATE TABLE  tkprof_table
(
 date_of_insert                     DATE
,cursor_num                         NUMBER
,depth                              NUMBER
,user_id                            NUMBER
,parse_cnt                          NUMBER
,parse_cpu                          NUMBER
,parse_elap                         NUMBER
,parse_disk                         NUMBER
,parse_query                        NUMBER
,parse_current                      NUMBER
,parse_miss                         NUMBER
,exe_count                          NUMBER
,exe_cpu                            NUMBER
,exe_elap                           NUMBER
,exe_disk                           NUMBER
,exe_query                          NUMBER
,exe_current                        NUMBER
,exe_miss                           NUMBER
,exe_rows                           NUMBER
,fetch_count                        NUMBER
,fetch_cpu                          NUMBER
,fetch_elap                         NUMBER
,fetch_disk                         NUMBER
,fetch_query                        NUMBER
,fetch_current                      NUMBER
,fetch_rows                         NUMBER
,ticks                              NUMBER
,sql_statement                      LONG
);
INSERT INTO tkprof_table values
(
  SYSDATE, 1, 0, 59, 0, 0, 0, 0, 0, 0, 0
, 1, 0, 192, 0, 0, 0, 1, 0
, 0, 0, 0, 0, 0, 0, 0, 4294966155
```

```
, 'alter session set sql_trace=true
');
INSERT INTO tkprof_table VALUES
(
  SYSDATE, 2, 1, 0, 1, 0, 1232, 0, 0, 0, 1
, 1, 0, 745, 0, 0, 0, 0, 0
, 1, 0, 115, 0, 3, 0, 1, 17866289
, 'select obj#,type#,ctime,mtime,stime,status,dataobj#,flags,oid$,
spare1, spare
2 from obj$ where owner#=:1 and name=:2 and namespace=:3
and(remoteowner=:4 or r
emoteowner is null and :4 is null)and(linkname=:5 or linkname is
null and :5 is
null)and(subname=:6 or subname is null and :6 is null)
');
INSERT INTO tkprof_table VALUES
(
  SYSDATE, 3, 1, 0, 1, 0, 1400, 0, 0, 0, 1
, 1, 0, 658, 0, 0, 0, 0, 0
, 1, 0, 131, 0, 3, 0, 1, 5463
, 'select
ts#,file#,block#,nvl(bobj#,0),nvl(tab#,0),intcols,nvl(clucols,0),
audit
$,flags,pctfree$,pctused$,initrans,maxtrans,rowcnt,blkcnt,empcnt,
avgspc,chncnt,a
vgrln,analyzetime,
samplesize,cols,property,nvl(degree,1),nvl(instances,1),avgsp
c_flb,flbcnt,kernelcols,nvl(trigflag,
0),nvl(spare1,0),nvl(spare2,0),spare4,spar
e6 from tab$ where obj#=:1
');
INSERT INTO tkprof_table VALUES
(
  SYSDATE, 4, 1, 0, 2, 0, 1110, 0, 0, 0, 1
, 2, 15625, 757, 0, 0, 0, 0, 0
, 2, 0, 221, 0, 6, 0, 2, 8966
, 'select
type#,blocks,extents,minexts,maxexts,extsize,extpct,user#,iniexts,
NVL(
lists,65535),NVL(groups,65535),cachehint,hwmincr, NVL(spare1,0)
from seg$ where
ts#=:1 and file#=:2 and block#=:3
');
INSERT INTO tkprof _table VALUES
(
  SYSDATE, 4, 1, 0, 1, 0, 1802, 0, 0, 0, 1
, 1, 0, 1089, 0, 0, 0, 0, 0
, 2, 0, 489, 0, 5, 0, 1, 23441
, 'select i.obj#,i.ts#,i.file#,i.block#,i.intcols,i.type#,i.flags,
i.property,i.
pctfree$,i.initrans,i.maxtrans,i.blevel,i.leafcnt,i.distkey,
i.lblkkey,i.dblkkey
,i.clufac,i.cols,i.analyzetime,i.samplesize,i.dataobj#,
nvl(i.degree,1),nvl(i.in
stances,1),i.rowcnt,mod(i.pctthres$,256),i.indmethod#,i.trunccnt,
nvl(c.unicols,0
),nvl(c.deferrable#+c.valid#,0),
nvl(i.spare1,i.intcols),i.spare4,spare2,spare6,
```

```
 decode(i.pctthres$,null,null, mod(trunc(i.pctthres$/256),256))
from ind$ i, (se
lect enabled, min(cols) unicols, min(to_number(bitand(defer,1)))
deferrable#, mi
n(to_number(bitand(defer,4))) valid# from cdef$ where obj#=:1 and
enabled > 1 gr
oup by enabled) c where i.obj#=c.enabled(+) and i.bo#=:1
');
INSERT INTO tkprof _table VALUES
(
  SYSDATE, 5, 1, 0, 1, 0, 910, 0, 0, 0, 1
, 1, 0, 573, 0, 0, 0, 0, 0
, 2, 0, 147, 0, 3, 0, 1, 5409
, 'select pos#,intcol#,col#,spare1,bo#,spare2 from icol$ where
obj#=:1
');
INSERT INTO tkprof _table VALUES
(
  SYSDATE, 6, 1, 0, 1, 15625, 1426, 0, 0, 0, 1
, 1, 0, 775, 0, 0, 0, 0, 0
, 6, 0, 1744, 0, 3, 0, 5, 10773
, 'select
name,intcol#,segcol#,type#,length,nvl(precision#,0),decode(type#,2,
nvl
(scale,-
127/*MAXSB1MINAL*/),178,scale,179,scale,180,scale,181,scale,182,
scale,18
3,scale,231,scale,0),null$,fixedstorage,nvl(deflength,0),default$,
rowid,col#,pro
perty,
nvl(charsetid,0),nvl(charsetform,0),spare1,spare2,nvl(spare3,0)
from col$
 where obj#=:1 order by intcol#
');
INSERT INTO tkprof _table VALUES
(
  SYSDATE, 8, 1, 0, 1, 0, 831, 0, 0, 0, 1
, 1, 0, 597, 0, 0, 0, 0, 0
, 1, 0, 59, 0, 1, 0, 0, 5736
, 'select con#,obj#,rcon#,enabled,nvl(defer,0) from cdef$ where
robj#=:1
');
INSERT INTO tkprof _table VALUES
(
  SYSDATE, 9, 1, 0, 1, 0, 973, 0, 0, 0, 1
, 1, 0, 650, 0, 0, 0, 0, 0
, 1, 0, 43, 0, 2, 0, 0, 5050
, 'select
con#,type#,condlength,intcols,robj#,rcon#,match#,refact,nvl(enabled
,0)
,rowid,cols,nvl(defer,0),mtime,nvl(spare1,0) from cdef$ where
obj#=:1
');
INSERT INTO tkprof _table VALUES
(
  SYSDATE, 1, 0, 59, 1, 31250, 58068, 1, 1, 0, 1
, 1, 0, 85, 0, 0, 0, 0, 0
, 2, 0, 37301, 3, 4, 0, 1, 39511
```

```
, ' select * from employee where emp_id = 87933
');
INSERT INTO tkprof _table VALUES
(
  SYSDATE, 2, 1, 0, 2, 0, 1122, 0, 0, 0, 1
, 2, 0, 672, 0, 0, 0, 0, 0
, 2, 0, 178, 0, 6, 0, 2, 12416444
, 'select
o.owner#,o.name,o.namespace,o.remoteowner,o.linkname,o.subname,
o.datao
bj#,o.flags from obj$ o where o.obj#=:1
');
INSERT INTO tkprof _table VALUES
(
  SYSDATE, 1, 0, 59, 1, 0, 353, 0, 0, 0, 1
, 1, 0, 148, 0, 0, 0, 0, 0
, 0, 0, 0, 0, 0, 0, 0, 1160
, 'alter session set sql_trace=false
');
```

This file contains the DDL to create the table as well as the data to load. If the table already exists, the error will be ignored when it tries to create the table again.

tkprof Command Line Options

tkprof provides many useful command line options that provide additional functionality for the DBA.

- ***print*** – Lists only the first *n* SQL statements in the output file. If nothing is specified, all statements will be listed. Use this option when the list needs to be limited to the "Top *n*" statements. This is useful when combined with a sorting option to enable the top *n* statements by CPU, or disk reads, or parses, etc.

- ***aggregate*** – When "Yes", *tkprof* will combine the statistics from multiple user executions of the same SQL statement.

When "No", the statistics will be listed each time the statement is executed.

- ***insert*** – Creates a file that will load the statistics into a table in the database for further processing. Choose this option if you want to perform any advanced analysis of the *tkprof* output.

- ***sys*** – Enables or disables the inclusion of SQL statements executed by the SYS user, including recursive SQL statements. The default is to enable.

- ***table*** – Used in the Explain Plan command (if specified) for Oracle to load data temporarily into an Oracle table. The user must specify the schema and table name for the plan table. If the table exists all rows will be deleted otherwise *tkprof* will create the table and use it.

- ***record*** - creates a SQL script with the specified filename that contains all non-recursive SQL statements from the trace file. For DBAs wanting to log the SQL statements in a separate file, this is the option to use. In the example earlier, the contents of the *Allsql.sql* file include:

```
alter session set sql_trace=true ;
select * from employee where emp_id = 87933 ;
alter session set sql_trace=false ;
```

- ***explain*** – Executes an Explain Plan for each statement in the trace file and displays the output. Explain Plan is less useful when used in conjunction with *tkprof* than it is when used alone. Explain Plan provides the *predicted* optimizer execution path without actually executing the statement. *tkprof* shows you the *actual* execution path and statistics after the statement is executed. In addition, running Explain Plan against SQL statements that were captured and saved is always problematic given dependencies and changes in the database environment.

- ***sort*** – Sorts the SQL statements in the trace file by the criteria deemed most important by the DBA. This option allows the DBA to view the SQL statements that consume the most resources at the top of the file, rather than searching the entire file contents for the poor performers. The following are the data elements available for sorting:

  - ***prscnt*** – The number of times the SQL was parsed.

  - ***prscpu*** – The CPU time spent parsing.

  - ***prsela*** – The elapsed time spent parsing the SQL.

  - ***prsdsk*** – The number of physical reads required for the parse.

- ***prsmis*** – The number of consistent block reads required for the parse.

- ***prscu*** - The number of current block reads required for the parse.

- ***execnt*** – The number of times the SQL statement was executed.

- ***execpu*** – The CPU time spent executing the SQL.

- ***exeela*** – The elapsed time spent executing the SQL.

- ***exedsk*** – The number of physical reads during execution.

- ***exeqry*** – The number of consistent block reads during execution.

- ***execu*** – The number of current block reads during execution.

- ***exerow*** – The number of rows processed during execution.

- ***exemis*** – The number of library cache misses during execution.

- ***fchcnt*** – The number of fetches performed.

- ***fchcpu*** – The CPU time spent fetching rows.

- ***fchela*** – The elapsed time spent fetching rows.

- ***fchdsk*** – The number of physical disk reads during the fetch.

- ***fchqry*** – The number of consistent block reads during the fetch.

- ***fchcu*** – The number of current block reads during the fetch.

- ***fchrow*** – The number of rows fetched for the query.

Many sort options exist, however some are more useful than others. *Execnt*, *execpu*, *exedsk* and *prscnt* are the most useful sort parameters when formatting trace output with *tkprof* because they are more indicative of most SQL performance issues. The execution counts are most indicative of performance issues and therefore should bubble to the top. In particular, this is true of the SQL statement that used the most CPU – *execpu*. The *prscnt* parameter is important because it shows the SQL statements that are parsed most, usually a result of not using bind variables.

SQL Execution Statistics in 9i

The SQL tuning process prior to 9.2 involved executing SQL commands, then OS commands, and then SQL commands again. This is a very time-consuming and burdensome process. In 9.2, Oracle decided to retain the SQL metrics for each statement in the SGA (library cache) while the statement remains cached. The DBA could then diagnose SQL issues at a SQL prompt and leave *tkprof* alone. This is a vast improvement over prior versions.

Oracle9.2 contains the following views that enable the DBA to identify SQL issues directly from a SQL prompt. These views should be used to periodically check SQL statistics and full-table scans, alerting the DBA to problem areas requiring corrective action.

- ***v$sql_plan*** - This view shows the same information as shown by Explain Plan except it is the actual execution plan and not the predicted one – just like *tkprof* and even better than Explain Plan.

- ***v$sql_plan_statistics*** - This view contains the execution statistics for each operation (step) in the *v$sql_plan*. Queries should access this view and look for poor SQL operations including *TABLE ACCESS FULL* – full-table scans.

- ***v$sql_plan_statistics_all*** - This view combines data from *v$sql_plan*, *v$sql_plan_statistics* and *v$sql_workarea*.

Both *v$sql_plan_statistics* and *v$sql_plan_statistics_all* are not populated by default. The option *statistics_level=all* must be set.

Best Practices for Using *tkprof*

Enable tracing only on those sessions that are having problems. Be selective to minimize the performance burden on the sessions and to retain more free space in the user dump destination directory.

Rename trace files after tracing is disabled. The new file name should be something more meaningful that will be recognizable at a later date. The name *employee_index.trc* is much more meaningful than *ORCL92_ora_3172.trc*.
Delete trace files that are no longer needed to reduce clutter and free disk space.

Explain Plan is not as useful when used in conjunction with *tkprof* since the trace file contains the actual execution path of the SQL statement. Use Explain Plan when anticipated execution statistics are desired without actually executing the statement.

When tracing a session, remember that nothing in *v$session* indicates that a session is being traced. Therefore, trace with caution and remember to disable tracing after an adequate amount of trace data has been generated.

tkprof does not control the contents of a trace file, it simply formats them. Oracle provides multiple ways to actually generate the trace file. *tkprof* is valuable for detailed trace file analysis. For those DBAs that pefer a simpler tracing mechanism with instant feedback, the *autotrace* utility should be used.

Simple Tracing With *autotrace*

The *autotrace* utility is a very underutilized feature of SQL*Plus. It offers statement tracing and instant feedback on any successful *SELECT*, *INSERT*, *UPDATE* or *DELETE* statement. The utility requires a plan table (for the Explain Plan) under the current user's schema. In addition, it requires the *plustrace* or DBA role for the user executing the trace. The source for the PLUSTRACE role can be found in $ORACLE_HOME/sqlplus/admin/plustrce.sql.

Tracing is enabled via the set *autotrace* command in SQL*Plus:

```
SQL> set autotrace on
SQL> select ename from emp where empno = 1122;

no rows selected

Execution Plan
----------------------------------------------------------
   0      SELECT STATEMENT Optimizer=CHOOSE
   1    0   TABLE ACCESS (BY INDEX ROWID) OF 'EMP'
   2    1     INDEX (UNIQUE SCAN) OF 'PK_EMP' (UNIQUE)


Statistics
----------------------------------------------------------
         83  recursive calls
          0  db block gets
```

```
 21  consistent gets
  3  physical reads
  0  redo size
221  bytes sent via SQL*Net to client
368  bytes received via SQL*Net from client
  1  SQL*Net roundtrips to/from client
  0  sorts (memory)
  0  sorts (disk)
  0  rows processed
```

autotrace provides instantaneous feedback including the returned rows, execution plan, and statistics. The user doesn't need to be concerned about trace file locations and formatting since the output is displayed instantly on the screen. This is very important data that can be used to tune the SQL statement.

autotrace supports the following options:

- **on** – Enables all options.
- **on explain** – Displays returned rows and the explain plan.
- **on statistics** – Displays returned rows and statistics.
- **trace explain** – Displays the execution plan for a select statement without actually executing it.

  ```
  set autotrace trace explain
  ```

- **traceonly** – Displays execution plan and statistics without displaying the returned rows. This option should be used when a large result set is expected.

autotrace is so easy to use that it should be the first tracing utility used for most SQL performance tuning issues. *tkprof* can be used for more detailed analysis.

For DBAs requiring the lowest level debugging – *oradebug*, described in the next section, will do the job.

Low Level Tracing With *oradebug*

The *oradebug* utility falls into the "hidden" classification of utilities due to the lack of available documentation. The utility is invoked directly from SQL*Plus beginning in version 8.1.5 and Server Manager in releases prior to that. The utility can trace a user session as well as perform many other, more global database tracing functions.

oradebug requires the SYSDBA privilege to execute (connect internal on older Oracle versions). The list of *oradebug* options can be viewed by typing *oradebug help* at the SQL*Plus prompt:

```
SQL> oradebug help
HELP           [command]                 Describe one or all commands
SETMYPID                                 Debug current process
SETOSPID       <ospid>                   Set OS pid of process to debug
SETORAPID      <orapid> ['force']        Set Oracle pid of process to debug
DUMP           <dump_name> <lvl> [addr]  Invoke named dump
DUMPSGA        [bytes]                   Dump fixed SGA
DUMPLIST                                 Print a list of available dumps
EVENT          <text>                    Set trace event in process
SESSION_EVENT  <text>                    Set trace event in session
DUMPVAR        <p|s|uga> <name> [level]  Print/dump a fixed PGA/SGA/UGA variable
SETVAR         <p|s|uga> <name> <value>  Modify a fixed PGA/SGA/UGA variable
PEEK           <addr> <len> [level]      Print/Dump memory
POKE           <addr> <len> <value>      Modify memory
WAKEUP         <orapid>                  Wake up Oracle process
SUSPEND                                  Suspend execution
RESUME                                   Resume execution
FLUSH                                    Flush pending writes to trace file
CLOSE_TRACE                              Close trace file
```

```
TRACEFILE_NAME                                  Get name of trace file
LKDEBUG                                         Invoke global enqueue service debugger
NSDBX                                           Invoke CGS name-service debugger
-G              <Inst-List | def | all>         Parallel oradebug command prefix
-R              <Inst-List | def | all>         Parallel oradebug prefix (return output
SETINST         <instance# .. | all>            Set instance list in double quotes
SGATOFILE       <SGA dump dir>          Dump SGA to file; dirname in double quotes
DMPCOWSGA       <SGA dump dir> Dump & map SGA as COW; dirname in double quotes
MAPCOWSGA       <SGA dump dir>          Map SGA as COW; dirname in double quotes
HANGanalyze     [level]                         Analyze system hang
FFBEGIN                                         Flash Freeze the Instance
FFDEREGISTER                                    FF deregister instance from cluster
FFTERMINST                                      Call exit and terminate instance
FFRESUMEINST                                    Resume the flash frozen instance
FFSTATUS                                        Flash freeze status of instance
SKDSTTPCS       <ifname>  <ofname>              Helps translate PCs to names
WATCH           <address> <len> <self|exist|all|target>  Watch a region of memory
DELETE          <local|global|target> watchpoint <id>    Delete a watchpoint
SHOW            <local|global|target> watchpoints        Show  watchpoints
CORE                                            Dump core without crashing process
UNLIMIT                                         Unlimit the size of the trace file
PROCSTAT                                        Dump process statistics
CALL            <func> [arg1] ... [argn]        Invoke function with arguments
```

Identical to *tkprof*, *oradebug* depends on trace files to store its output. These files are in the same location as specified by the *user_dump_dest* initialization parameter. The trace files are named according to the SPID of the process where the *oradebug* command is executed – the same naming scheme as described earlier.

Some of the *oradebug* options apply to a particular session and therefore require a system process id (*SPID*) as obtained from *v$process*. Other options are more global in nature and can be executed without attaching to any session.

ORADEBUG Session Trace

The *oradebug* utility provides the ability to trace a particular user session. In addition, *oradebug* provides additional details that are not available through other tracing mechanisms.

The following steps are required to trace a user session with *oradebug*:

1. Obtain the *SPID* from *v$process*.

```
SQL> select username, spid from v$process;
```

2. Start the debug session with the SPID of the process that needs traced.

```
SQL> oradebug setospid 2280
```

3. Select the appropriate trace level. There are four different options when specifying a tracing level:

   - **Level 1** – provides "base set" tracing information. Bind variables are displayed as variables (:b1).

   - **Level 4** – provides Level 1 data and the actual data values of bind variables.

   - **Level 8** – provides Level 1 data and information on wait events when the elapsed time is greater than the CPU time.

   - **Level 12** – combines levels 1, 4 and 8 tracing information. A Level 12 trace contains base set, bind variable values and wait events.

   The oradebug command below will enable the maximum tracing possible:

```
SQL> oradebug event 10046 trace name context forever, level
12
```

4. Turn tracing off.

```
SQL> oradebug event 10046 trace name context off
```

5. **Obtain the trace file name.** The *oradebug* facility provides an easy way to obtain the file name:

```
SQL> oradebug tracefile_name
c:\oracle9i\admin\ORCL92\udump\mooracle_ora_2280.trc
```

6. Format the trace file with *tkprof* (as described in the earlier section on *tkprof*).

The result will be a trace file that contains more trace file information. Viewing wait events and bind variable values can be critical to diagnosing performance issues.

ORADEBUG Dumps

The *oradebug* utility provides many options for dumping database information to trace files. In order to know what data can be dumped, the *dumplist* command will return the available options.

```
EVENTS                  GRANULELIST        TR_RESET_NORMAL
TRACE_BUFFER_ON         GRANULELISTCHK     TEST_DB_ROBUSTNESS
TRACE_BUFFER_OFF        SCOREBOARD         LOCKS
HANGanalyze             GES_STATE          GC_ELEMENTS
LATCHES                 ADJUST_SCN         FILE_HDRS
PROCESSSTATE            NEXT_SCN_WRAP      KRB_CORRUPT_INTERVAL
SYSTEMSTATE             CONTROLF           KRB_CORRUPT_SIZE
INSTANTIATIONSTATE      FULL_DUMPS         KRB_PIECE_FAIL
REFRESH_OS_STATS        BUFFERS            KRB_OPTIONS
CROSSIC                 RECOVERY           KRB_SIMULATE_NODE_AFFINITY
CONTEXTAREA             SET_TSN_P1         KRB_TRACE
HEAPDUMP                BUFFER             KRB_BSET_DAYS
HEAPDUMP_ADDR           PIN_BLOCKS         DROP_SEGMENTS
POKE_ADDRESS            BC_SANITY_CHECK    TREEDUMP
POKE_LENGTH             FLUSH_CACHE        LONGF_CREATE
POKE_VALUE              LOGHIST            ROW_CACHE
POKE_VALUE0             ARCHIVE_ERROR      LIBRARY_CACHE
GLOBAL_AREA             REDOHDR            SHARED_SERVER_STATE
MEMORY_LOG              LOGERROR           KXFPCLEARSTATS
REALFREEDUMP            OPEN_FILES         KXFPDUMPTRACE
ERRORSTACK              DATA_ERR_ON        KXFPBLATCHTEST
HANGANALYZE_PROC        DATA_ERR_OFF       KXFXSLAVESTATE
TEST_STACK_DUMP         BLK0_FMTCHG        KXFXCURSORSTATE
```

BG_MESSAGES ENQUEUES SIMULATE_EOV KSFQP_LIMIT KSKDUMPTRACE DBSCHEDULER	TR_SET_BLOCK TR_SET_ALL_BLOCKS TR_SET_SIDE TR_CRASH_AFTER_WRITE TR_READ_ONE_SIDE TR_CORRUPT_ONE_SIDE	WORKAREATAB_DUMP OBJECT_CACHE SAVEPOINTS OLAP_DUMP

One scenario in which a dump may aid in diagnosing the problem is when dealing with a system hang. If no errors exist in the alert log and the database appears to be hung, connect as SYSDBA and execute the following:

```
SQL> oradebug setmypid
SQL> oradebug unlimit
SQL> oradebug dump systemstate 10
```

This creates a very large trace file from the system dump. For this reason, the *oradebug unlimit* option should be used to override the maximum trace file size as specified in *init.ora.*

oradebug also has the capability to only produce trace output if a particular error is encountered. This command is especially useful when certain errors are encountered inconsistently. Rather than generate enormous trace files, the trace data will only be generated when the particular error occurs. The following command will monitor a particular session and only generate trace data when the ORA-00942 error is hit:

```
SQL> oradebug event 942 trace name errorstack level 3
```

oradebug can also be used to *suspend* and *resume* any user database connection. When suspended, the user session will simply hang until the resume command is processed. During the suspension period, *v$session_wait* will indicate that the session is waiting on the debugger.

Only a few of the *oradebug* options were discussed. *oradebug* is a powerful utility to be used only by expert DBAs when diagnosing serious database issues. *oradebug* can be used in tandem with *tkprof* to get more detailed information in trace files. In addition, the tool can be used to generate system or process state dumps which can be vital when diagnosing system hang scenarios.

The last tracing utility to be explained in this chapter is tightly coupled with the OEM product – Oracle Trace.

The Oracle Trace Utility

Oracle Trace (*otrccl*) is a data collection utility used mainly with Oracle Enterprise Manager. However, the command line API can be used with any software to gather data for performance tuning. Oracle Trace collects the following types of data:

- SQL statements and their execution statistics
- SQL Execution plan statistics
- Logical and physical database transactions
- Resource Usage for each database event – CPU time and I/O.

Before Oracle Trace can be started, the environment must be configured. The *show_parameter* command can be used from SQL*Plus to display all of the Oracle Trace parameters.

```
SQL> show parameter oracle_trace

NAME                                 TYPE        VALUE
------------------------------------ ----------- ------------------------------
oracle_trace_collection_name         string
oracle_trace_collection_path         string      %ORACLE_HOME%\OTRACE\ADMIN\CDF\
oracle_trace_collection_size         integer     5242880
oracle_trace_enable                  boolean     TRUE
oracle_trace_facility_name           string      oracled
oracle_trace_facility_path           string      %ORACLE_HOME%\OTRACE\ADMIN\FDF\
```

The Oracle Trace instance parameters include the following:

- ***oracle_trace_collection_name*** - The name of a set of collection statistics – one collection run. This is an optional parameter that can only be changed in the configuration file and not with an ALTER SYSTEM command. There is really no benefit to having this set in the *init.ora* since it can be performed more easily with methods described later in this section.

- ***oracle_trace_collection_path*** – Specifies the path where the Oracle Trace *.cdf* and .dat files are located.

- ***oracle_trace_collection_size*** – Specifies, in bytes, the maximum size that the collection file can be. The default is 5242880.

- ***oracle_trace_enable*** – (True | False) When true, this enables Oracle Trace to be executed against the instance. A value of true doesn't mean that tracing is active.

Instead, it means that tracing can be activated.

- ***oracle_trace_facility_name*** – Specifies the Oracle Trace product definition file - *.fdf* file to use. The default is *Oracled.fdf*.

- ***oracle_trace_facility_path*** – The directory where the Oracle Trace definition files are located.

In the Oracle Trace Admin directory (*$ORACLE_HOME/otrace/admin*), the following files should be present as required by Oracle Trace – *regid.dat*, *process.dat* and *collect.dat*. If these files are not there, execute the *otrccref* executable (in $ORACLE_HOME\bin) to create them.

Starting Oracle Trace

Once *oracle_trace_enable=true*, tracing can be activated. When tracing is active, the current sessions will be logged. The *otrccol* executable is used to start Oracle Trace and requires a *job_id* and an *input* parameter file. Any number can be specified for the *job_id*, but the input file must contain certain tags.

```
otrccol start 1 otrace_input_file
```

The contents of *otrace_input_file* are:

```
col_name=test_collection
dat_file=test_collection.dat
cdf_file=test_collection.cdf
fdf_file=ORACLED.fdf
regid=1 192216243 0 0 5 ORCL92
```

The *col_name* is the name of the collection determined by the person initiating the trace. The *dat_file* and *cdf_file* parameters are simply the files that will be used by Oracle Trace to store internal information. For consistency, use the same name as specified in the *col_name* and add the appropriate file extension (*.dat* and *.cdf*). The *fdf_file* parameter specifies the facility name to be used by Oracle Trace and maps to a server the event specified by the user. The server event sets that can be used as values for the *fdf_file* are ORACLE, ORACLEC, ORACLED, ORACLEE, and ORACLESM. And finally, the *reg_id* parameter is always the number 1 192216243 0 0 5 concatenated with the SID of the database.

Oracle Trace Server Event Sets

- **ORACLE** – collects all statistics, including wait events.
- **ORACLEC** – the Cache I/O event set that collects buffer cache I/O statistics.
- **ORACLED** – the default server event set that collects statistics for the database.
- **ORACLEE** – the expert event set that collects statistics for the Oracle Expert tool in OEM.

- **ORACLESM** – the summary event set that collects statistics for the Summary Advisor application.

Enabling tracing will create two files in the directory specified for *oracle_trace_collection_path*. It uses the collection name as part of the file name:

```
   54,243 test_collection.cdf
5,433,236 test_collection.dat
```

The *.cdf* file contains collection profile information while the *.dat* file holds the binary trace data. The *.dat* file can become extremely large depending on the amount of time tracing is enabled.

Stopping Oracle Trace

When the DBA decides tracing has run long enough, it can be stopped by:

```
otrccol stop 1 otrace_stop_file
```

The number (1) is the *job_id* that matches the one used in the start command. The contents of *otrace_stop_file* include the cdf file name along with the collection name.

```
cdf_file=test_collection.cdf
col_name=test_collection
```

Reporting Tracing Results

The *otrcrep* executable is used to format the trace file results to a file. The minimum requirement for the *otcrep* utility is the cdf file name.

```
otrcrep test_collection.cdf
```

Oracle Trace generated many .txt files in the current working directory.

```
10,456,044  test_collection.txt
   938,166  test_collectioncacheIO.txt
     1,087  test_collectionErrorStack.txt
 1,993,638  test_collectionExecute.txt
 1,990,157  test_collectionFetch.txt
    62,151  test_collectionLogicalTX.txt
 2,043,251  test_collectionParse.txt
    63,951  test_collectionPhysicalTX.txt
       148  test_collectionPROCESS.txt
 1,869,186  test_collectionRowSource.txt
 1,162,699  test_collectionSQLSegment.txt
   675,929  test_collectionWait.txt
```

21.2 MB of data was generated when two simple statements were executed from one connected session in SQL*Plus.

The rest of the command line options for *otrcrep* include:

- ***Output_path*** – output directory for generated files. If not specified, Oracle Trace will use the current directory.

- ***-p*** – creates a report for a specific process obtained from the PROCESS.TXT report. Below is an example of the contents of PROCESS.TXT. This option should be used to pinpoint sessions that need analysis.

```
30-DEC-02 19:55:54         Oracle Trace Detail Report
Page1
Collection:test_collection                                  Oracle Trace
V9.2

 Epid      User Nam  CPU Type  OS Version  Node Name  Timestamp

 2308      SYSTEM    MOOREPC   Windows NT  MOOREPC    30-DEC-02 19:30:29.920

 2308      5      9.2          30-DEC-02 19:30:29.936  ORCL92
```

- ***-w*** – sets the width of the report. The default is 80 characters.

- ***-l*** – sets the number of lines per page. The default is 63 lines.

- ***-h*** – suppresses all event and item report headers resulting in a much smaller report.

- ***-a*** – creates a report containing all of the events combined into one file. Beware when using this option since a great deal of output will be generated.

Other than *process.txt*, the *.txt* files themselves are very difficult to interpret. For example, a partial listing from *testCollectionExecute.txt.* is shown below.

```
Event:Execute   Product:oracle   Version:9.2

 2308       19:30:34.342            8           1          207888
 3248896      1767193     1226573     1603899     199         886969
 189759504    1813758     7056        0           1896        0
 0            1           127735      10163       0           0
 0            0           0           0           0           0
 0            3223513021  0

 2308       19:30:34.342            8           1          207888
 3248896      1767193     1226573     1603899     199         886969
 189759504    1813758     7056        0           1896        0
 0            1           1       1       0          3223513021
 0000000012f0d374  127735      10163       0           0           0
```

There's not much information in this file that is easily decipherable. The next step involves loading this data into the database so that the DBA can query the tables to get exactly the information needed.

Loading Trace Data into the Database

Although this step is technically optional, it is required in order to get data in a useful format that is understandable. The command to load the data into the database is:

```
otrccol format otrace_format_file
```

The contents of *otrace_format_file* include:

```
username=scott
password=tiger
service=ORCL92
cdf_file=test_collection.cdf
full_format=0
```

All of the parameters above have been explained except *full_format*. The options for full format include 0 (partial format) or 1 (full format).

Oracle creates the following named tables in the database to be used by Oracle Trace. Based on the naming scheme, it is clear that Oracle designed these tables for internal use only, to be used with Oracle tools. These tables will be created automatically if they don't already exist in the schema of the connected user, defined by the username parameter.

```
V_192216243_F_5_E_10_9_2
V_192216243_F_5_E_11_9_2
V_192216243_F_5_E_12_9_2
V_192216243_F_5_E_13_9_2
V_192216243_F_5_E_14_9_2
V_192216243_F_5_E_15_9_2
V_192216243_F_5_E_16_9_2
V_192216243_F_5_E_17_9_2
V_192216243_F_5_E_1_9_2
V_192216243_F_5_E_2_9_2
V_192216243_F_5_E_3_9_2
V_192216243_F_5_E_4_9_2
V_192216243_F_5_E_5_9_2
V_192216243_F_5_E_6_9_2
```

```
V_192216243_F_5_E_7_9_2
V_192216243_F_5_E_8_9_2
V_192216243_F_5_E_9_9_2
```

Oracle provides many SQL scripts that access these tables and provide meaningful data, including wait events, logical transactions per second, sorts, and more. These scripts are located in the *$ORACLE_HOME/otrace/demo* directory. The *otrcsyn.sql* script can be executed to create meaningful synonyms for the tables above.

Oracle Corporation provides tools that access and display the data generated by Oracle Trace, including Trace Data Viewer (Figure 5.2) within OEM.

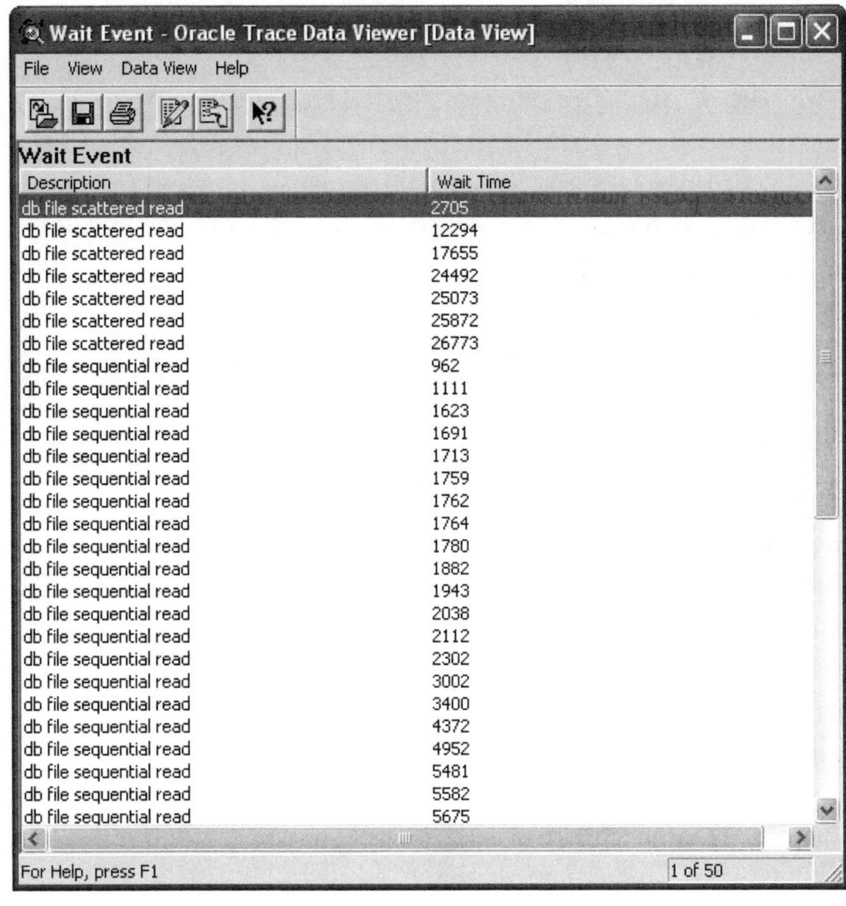

Figure 5.2 – Trace Data Viewer in OEM

Deleting Trace Data

There are two places from which trace data needs to be deleted. The first is the generated *cdf* and *dat* files. The *otrccol* command is used with an argument of *dcf*, along with the collection name and name of the *cdf* file. This will not delete the *.txt* files produced by the *otrcrep* executable – those will need to be deleted manually.

```
otrccol dcf test_collection test_collection.cdf
```

The data also needs to be deleted. The *otrccol* command is used again, this time specifying *dfd*, the collection name, and connection information for the database.

```
otrccol dfd test_collection scott tiger ORCL92
```

otrccol, *otrcrep*, *otrcref* and *otrcfmt* are all executables of the Oracle Trace utility. Different components within Oracle Enterprise Manager (Oracle Expert, Oracle Trace Data Viewer) access and display the information generated by Oracle Trace. However, Oracle Trace has lost its usefulness with the progression of tools like *bstat/estat*, *oradebug*, Statspack and *tkprof*. These alternatives provide much of the same information as Oracle Trace while proving to be much easier to use.

Oracle Trace has a limited future while Trace Analyzer is just beginning.

Trace Analyzer

Oracle has provided another utility initially designed for performance tuning Oracle Applications. Trace Analyzer is provided in the form of a PL/SQL package (TRCA$). The Trace Analyzer utility is available via download on the Oracle Metalink web site. This utility supports only version 8.1.6 and above due the requirement of being able to read OS files from PL/SQL into the database.

How it Works

Trace Analyzer requires that a one-time configuration be performed. During this configuration, many objects are installed in the database to serve as a tracing repository. Once downloaded from Metalink and installed, a SQL script can be executed passing in the name of the trace file. Trace Analyzer will then read the trace file and provide useful statistical information. The trace file used by Trace Analyzer is the same *.trc* file generated by any session trace.

On installation, Trace Analyzer creates the following SQL files. These can be installed locally on a client PC or on the database server itself.

- TRCACREA.sql - creates all objects needed by Trace Analyzer by calling other scripts below.
- TRCADROP.sql - drops the schema objects.
- TRCAPKGB.sql - creates the package body.
- TRCAPKGS.sql - creates the package header (specification).
- TRCAREPO.sql - creates the staging repository.
- TRCADIRA.sql - creates the directory object pointing to the place where the trace files

exist (only if placing traces on a directory other than *user_dump_dest*).

- TRCAGRNT.sql - grants privileges needed to use Trace Analyzer
- TRCAREVK.sql - revokes privileges granted by TRCAGRNT.
- TRCAPURG.sql - purges old SQL traces from the repository.
- TRCATRNC.sql - truncates the staging repository.
- TRCANLZR.sql - main Trace Analyzer script that generates the report.
- TRCACRSR.sql - generates report for one cursor.
- TRCAEXEC.sql - generates report for one cursor execution.

Executing Trace Analyzer

First, tracing needs enabled at the appropriate level. For example, to provide maximum trace data, a Level 12 trace can be started for the current session:

```
SQL> ALTER SESSION SET EVENTS '10046 TRACE NAME CONTEXT FOREVER,
LEVEL 12';
```

After the session executes for enough time to gain needed data, the trcanlzr SQL script can be executed. It requires the name of the directory object. This object points to the physical operating system directory for the *user_dump_dest*. The installation of the utility will automatically create the directory object required (named UDUMP).

```
SQL>@d:\trcanlzr.sql UDUMP asg920xr_ora_13033.trc
```

Once executed, the output will be displayed on the screen and a spool file is created.

Better than *tkprof*?

Traditionally, *tkprof* has been the best tracing diagnostics tool available. That is, until the introduction of Trace Analyzer which is everything *tkprof* is and more. However, as of version 9.2, the Trace Analyzer utility is still not shipped with the Oracle DBMS like *tkprof*.

Given access to both utilities, Trace Analyzer has the following advantages:

1. **Trace Analyzer provides the actual values of the bind variables in SQL.** No longer are DBAs faced with wondering what the values were at runtime – Trace Analyzer provides them.

   For the following SQL statement listed in the output:

```
DELETE FROM HISTORY where ALERT_TIME <= :b1  AND INSTANCE_NUMBER = :b2
```

Trace Analyzer would also display:

```
0:"2/4/2003 15:57:35" 1:1
```

which equates to the actual SQL statement of:

```
DELETE FROM HISTORY where ALERT_TIME <= :"2/4/2003 15:57:35" AND
INSTANCE_NUMBER = 1
```

2. **Trace Analyzer provides the hottest blocks, optimizer statistics for indexes and tables, and other information not available through *tkprof*.** The output below shows the SQL statement, the execution plan, and statistics for each object in the SQL.

```
DELETE FROM SCOTT.EMPLOYEE

call      count     cpu    elapsed      disk      query  current          rows     misses
------- ------- -------  --------- -------- --------- ---------  ------------ ---------
Parse       1     0.00     0.00       0          0         0             0         0
Execute     3     0.05     0.52       0         27       224           216         0
------- -------- --------  -------- -------- --------- ---------   ----------- --------
total       4     0.05     0.52       0         27       224           216         0

Explain Plan
---------------------------------------------------------------
...3 DELETE STATEMENT
...2 .DELETE OF 'SCOTT.EMPLOYEE
...1 ..TABLE ACCESS (FULL) OF 'SCOTT.EMPLOYEE'

OWNER.TABLE_NAME
...owner.index_name                    num rows     blocks     sample last analyzed date
------------------------------------ ---------- ---------- ---------- -------------------
SCOTT.EMPLOYEE..........................
```

The output above indicates that the EMPLOYEE table does not have statistics.

3. **Trace Analyzer separates user recursive and internal recursive calls, unlike *tkprof*.**

4. **Trace Analyzer provides more detailed wait event information, which can be very useful to those DBAs who prefer wait-based tuning methodologies.** This data is

also very helpful when there is a significant gap between CPU and elapsed times.

```
Event                                       Times     Count     Max.     Total    Blocks
waited on                                  Waited  Zero Time   Wait     Waited  Accessed
----------------------------------------- --------- --------- -------  ------- --------
PL/SQL lock timer.......................       15         0     5.01     75.08
log file sync...........................        1         0     0.01      0.01
library cache pin.......................        1         0     0.00      0.00
SQL*Net message from client (idle).......       2         0    17.22     30.21
SQL*Net message to client (idle).........       3         0     0.00      0.00
total...................................       22         0    17.22    105.30        0
```

One drawback concerning Trace Analyzer is that it requires objects in the database (the tracing repository) and that means more configuration work on each database that needs the utility installed. This is unlike *tkprof*, which is an executable file always there, ready to serve.

The benefits of the Trace Analyzer far outweigh the negatives since never before has so much useful information been available to the Oracle tuner in one place. Usually, *tkprof* needs combined with *statspack* reports and other utilities provide a comprehensive picture. Trace Analyzer takes tuning to a new level.

Summary

This chapter has discussed many useful utilities that can be used to trace database activity. Tracing is an important tool used to detect bottlenecks and improve Oracle database performance. Basic SQL analysis and tuning can be performed by the *autotrace* utility in SQL*Plus. For more detailed analysis, certain system commands will generate trace output that can be transformed by *tkprof* or

Trace Analyzer. *oradebug* provides an additional tracing capability both at the system and session level and it's output is also a trace file that can be formatted by *tkprof.* And, although available for use, the Oracle Trace utility is used mainly by the OEM product from Oracle.

The most comprehensive of all Oracle tracing utilities is one that is not yet provided with the database. Trace Analyzer is an extremely useful PL/SQL package that provides a gold mine of diagnostic information.

Shifting gears from tuning to networking, the next chapter will discuss the Oracle utilities available for database network administration.

Chapter 7

Networking Utilities

The utilities discussed in this chapter are those that assist the DBA in addressing networking and connectivity issues. The Oracle database may be perfectly tuned, but if the user cannot connect to it, the database is useless. Utilities such as *tnsping*, *trcroute*, *traceroute*, *lsnrctl*, *ping*, *trcasst*, and *tracert* will be covered in this chapter.

Managing Listeners with *lsnrctl*

The *lsnrctl* utility manages the Oracle listener processes. The Oracle listener process is required for database applications to access the database through SQL*Net or Net8. *lsnrctl* requires entries in the *listener.ora* file that specify the port for that listener. The *listener.ora* file is the configuration file for the network listener. It resides on the server and defines the network listener address, the SID for the database for which it listens, and other optional parameters for tracing and logging.

The *lsnrctl* command can be executed without parameters, in which the *lsnrctl* shell will be invoked, or it can execute commands directly when specified on the command line.

```
$ lsnrctl

LSNRCTL for Solaris: Version 9.2.0.1.0 - Production on 30-JAN-2003
11:54:13

(c) Copyright 1998 Oracle Corporation.  All rights reserved.

Welcome to LSNRCTL, type "help" for information.
LSNRCTL> help
The following operations are available
An asterisk (*) denotes a modifier or extended command:

start               stop                status
services            version             reload
save_config         trace               spawn
dbsnmp_start        dbsnmp_stop         dbsnmp_status
change_password     quit                exit
set*                show*
```

The following commands are used to manage the listener:

- ***start*** – Starts the listener with the name specified, otherwise LISTENER will be used. For Windows systems, the listener can also be started from the Control Panel.

- ***stop*** – Stops the listener. For Windows systems, the listener can also be stopped from the Control Panel.

- ***status*** – Provides status information about the listener, including start date, uptime, and trace level.

- ***services*** – Displays each service available, along with the connection history.

- ***version*** – Displays the version information of the listener.

- ***reload*** – Forces a read of the configuration file in order for new settings to take effect without stopping and starting the listener.

- ***save_config*** – Creates a backup of the existing *listener.ora* file and saves changes to the current version.

- ***trace*** – Sets the trace level to one of the following – OFF, USER, ADMIN, or SUPPORT.

- ***spawn*** – Spawns a program that runs with an alias in the *listener.ora* file.

- ***dbsnmp_start*** – Starts the DBSNMP subagent.

- ***dbsnmp_stop*** – Stops the DBSNMP subagent.

- ***dbsnmp_status*** – Displays the status of the DBSNMP subagent.

- ***change_password*** – Sets a new password for the listener.

- ***quit*** and ***exit*** – Exits the utility.

- ***set*** – Changes the value of any parameter. Everything that can be shown can be set.

- ***show*** – Displays current parameter settings.

```
LSNRCTL> show
The following operations are available after show
An asterisk (*) denotes a modifier or extended command:

rawmode                 displaymode             trc_file
trc_directory           trc_level               log_file
log_directory           log_status              current_listener
startup_waittime        snmp_visible            save_config_on_stop
```

Any of the above options can be shown (with the show command) or set.

The *start* command will start the default listener (named LISTENER); otherwise the name can be specified as the second parameter. Once started, the status can be determined using the *status* command:

```
LSNRCTL> status
Connecting to (ADDRESS=(PROTOCOL=tcp)(PORT=1521))
STATUS of the LISTENER
------------------------
Alias                     GRACELANV8_LSNR
Version                   TNSLSNR for Solaris: Version 9.0.1.0.0 -
Production
Start Date                07-NOV-2002 18:15:39
Uptime                    84 days 19 hr. 45 min. 18 sec
Trace Level               off
Security                  OFF
SNMP                      OFF
Listener Parameter File   /var/opt/oracle/listener.ora
Listener Log File
/usr/oracle/9.0.1/network/log/gracelanv8_lsnr.log
Listening Endpoints Summary...

(DESCRIPTION=(ADDRESS=(PROTOCOL=tcp)(HOST=gracelan.bmc.com)(PORT=15
21)))
(DESCRIPTION=(ADDRESS=(PROTOCOL=tcp)(HOST=gracelan.bmc.com)(PORT=15
25)))  (DESCRIPTION=(ADDRESS=(PROTOCOL=ipc)(KEY=EXTPROC)))
(DESCRIPTION=(ADDRESS=(PROTOCOL=tcp)(HOST=172.18.16.215)(PORT=8080)
)(PRESENTATION=http://admin)(SESSION=RAW))
(DESCRIPTION=(ADDRESS=(PROTOCOL=tcps)(HOST=172.18.16.215)(PORT=9090
))(PRESENTATION=http://admin)(SESSION=RAW))
Services Summary...
Service "GRA901m" has 1 instance(s).
  Instance "GRA901m", status UNKNOWN, has 1 handler(s) for this
service...
Service "GRA901m.world" has 1 instance(s).
  Instance "GRA901m", status READY, has 1 handler(s) for this
service...
Service "PLSExtProc" has 1 instance(s).
```

```
  Instance "PLSExtProc", status UNKNOWN, has 1 handler(s) for this
service...
The command completed successfully
```

The status shows a great deal information, including the uptime, trace level, and logs files. In addition, the status option displays the file in which the parameters for the listener are defined, */var/opt/oracle/listener.ora*.

Testing Connectivity

The three main things to check for when diagnosing remote database connection problems are the machine, the listener, and the database. The utilities that can be used to test each one of these include *ping*, *tnsping*, and a database connection, as depicted in Figure 7.1.

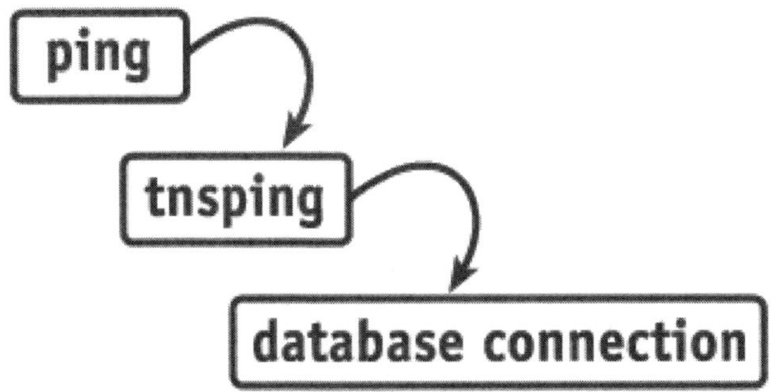

Figure 7.1 – Connectivity Testing Sequence

The *ping* utility is used to test the connectivity to a remote machine. *ping* will indicate whether a remote server is accessible and responding. If the ping command indicates that a machine cannot be accessed, the other connectivity tests will also fail.

The *ping* utility is usually found in */usr/sbin* on UNIX machines and simply reports the health of the remote machine specified:

```
$ ping asgard
asgard is alive
```

Used with the –s option, *ping* will show the packets received and timing information.

```
oracle@asgard:/usr/sbin > ping -s grace

PING gracelan: 56 data bytes
64 bytes from grace.bmc.com (172.18.16.215): icmp_seq=0. time=0. ms
64 bytes from grace.bmc.com (172.18.16.215): icmp_seq=1. time=0. ms
64 bytes from grace.bmc.com (172.18.16.215): icmp_seq=2. time=2. ms
64 bytes from grace.bmc.com (172.18.16.215): icmp_seq=3. time=0. ms
64 bytes from grace.bmc.com (172.18.16.215): icmp_seq=4. time=0. ms
64 bytes from grace.bmc.com (172.18.16.215): icmp_seq=5. time=0. ms

----gracelan PING Statistics----
6 packets transmitted, 6 packets received, 0% packet loss
round-trip (ms)  min/avg/max = 0/0/2
```

The *ping* command can also be executed at the DOS prompt on Windows machines to test client-to-server connectivity:

```
D:\> ping asgard

Pinging asgard.bmc.com [198.64.245.67] with 32 bytes of data:

Reply from 198.64.245.67: bytes=32 time<10ms TTL=254
Reply from 198.64.245.67: bytes=32 time<10ms TTL=254
Reply from 198.64.245.67: bytes=32 time<10ms TTL=254
Reply from 198.64.245.67: bytes=32 time<10ms TTL=254
```

Once connectivity to the host is confirmed with *ping*, the next connection to test is the listener. The *tnsping* utility is used to determine whether or not an Oracle service can be successfully reached. If a connection can be established from a client to a server (or server to server), *tnsping* will report the number of milliseconds it took to reach the remote service. If unsuccessful, a network error will be displayed. However, *tnsping* will only report if the listener process is up and provides no indication of the state of the database.

```
$ tnsping <net service name> <count>
```

The "net service name" must exist in the *tnsnames.ora* file. This file is used by clients and database servers to identify server destinations. It stores the service names and database addresses. The "count" parameter is optional and will show the number of times the command should try to connect to the specified service name.

```
$ tnsping GRACELANV8_GRA901m 5

TNS Ping Utility for Solaris: Version 9.2.0.1.0 - Production on 03-
JAN-2003 14:47:09

Copyright (c) 1997 Oracle Corporation.  All rights reserved.

Used parameter files:
/usr/oracle/9.2.0/network/admin/sqlnet.ora

Used TNSNAMES adapter to resolve the alias
Attempting to contact (DESCRIPTION= (ADDRESS= (PROTOCOL=TCP)
(HOST=gracelan)
(PORT=1525)) (CONNECT_DATA= (SID=GRA901m)))
OK (80 msec)
OK (10 msec)
OK (10 msec)
OK (0 msec)
OK (10 msec)
```

The result from the *tnsping* command above shows 80 milliseconds (ms) were required for the first "ping". During this time period, the alias GRACELANV8_GRA901m from the local *tnsnames.ora* file was retrieved, a DNS of the host "gracelan" was resolved, and the TNS connect and

refuse packets were transported. The second trip took only 10 ms because all of the connection information was already cached.

tnsping can be used to test listener connectivity but not database performance. While *ping* usually returns faster than *tnsping*, it gives no indication whether or not SQL*Net is performing. The *ping* utility simply uses IP to try to reach a destination, whereas *tnsping* uses TCP (a socket) and transfers data between two nodes. As a result, the *ping* utility will always be faster. A slow *tnsping* round trip could indicate any number of problems, including a very active server or a slow network.

To reach an Oracle Names Server with *tnsping*, the command can be formatted as shown below:

```
$ tnsping '(ADDRESS=(PROTOCOL=tcp)(HOST=onames-server)(PORT=1575))'
```

Once the host and listener connectivity have been verified, the final connectivity test is the database itself. The host could be accessible and the listener active, yet the database might still be inaccessible. Granted, this final test could be performed first and the others (*ping*, *tnsping*) performed only if this test fails, since if the database is accessible, so are the database host and listener. Any type of database connection can be used to confirm database connectivity (SQL*Plus, JDBC, ODBC, Pro*C).

The Java program (*ConnectionTest.java*) will parse a *tnsnames.ora* file and display the connectivity status of every entry in the file. It does this by establishing a JDBC connection with each entry in the file. The *tnsnames.ora* file must be in the same directory as the Java program in order to be found and parsed. In addition, the program requires that the same username and password be used for all connections.

ConnectionTest.java (not listed – See online code depot)

The Java program can be used to regularly monitor the availability of all databases in the *tnsnames.ora* file. It requires that the JDBC driver be listed in the CLASSPATH.

The *tnsnames.ora* entries are typically in the following format and are easily parsed by *ConnectionTest.java*:

```
ASGARDV8_ASG817t= (DESCRIPTION=
                    (ADDRESS=
                      (PROTOCOL=TCP)
                      (HOST=asgard)
                      (PORT=1525)
                    )
                    (CONNECT_DATA=
                      (SID=ASG817t)
                    )
                  )
```

When the program is executed, it will display the status of each connection listed in the file:

```
$java ConnectionTest system manager


FENRISV8_FEN920wa        Successful
MINOTAURV8_MIN817wa      Unsuccessful
MINOTAURV8_MIN8173x      Successful
NT817LEE                 Successful
```

```
ANGUSV8_ANG817us        Successful
JARAIXV8_AIX817r        Successful
ASGARDV8_ASG806r        Successful
```

Each entry in the file takes between 3 and 5 seconds to process. This may or may not be feasible in environments with many entries to test.

Tracing Listener Connections

Network connections are traced to provide a detailed description of the operations performed by Oracle's internal components. The trace data is stored in an output trace file that can then be analyzed.

The following four steps can be performed to trace listener connections:

1. Enable tracing for the appropriate period of time needed to capture enough data.

```
LSNRCTL> set trc_level ADMIN
```

2. Disable tracing.

```
LSNRCTL> set trc_level OFF
```

3. **View trace file (optional) - the trace file can be viewed although it is very cryptic.** The file can be located by using the *show* command along with *trc_directory* and again with *trc_file*. The following is an example of the raw trace file.

```
nsdo: cid=6, opcode=65, *bl=0, *what=0, uflgs=0x0, cflgs=0x2
nsdo: rank=64, nsctxrnk=0
nsdo: nsctx: state=7, flg=0x4200, mvd=0
nsdo: nsctxrnk=0
nsanswer: deferring connect attempt; at stage 5
```

```
nsevreg: begin registration process for 6
nsevreg: sgt=0, evn=4, evt[2]=0x0
nsevreg: begin notification process for 6
nsrah: setting transport read mode (2)
nsevreg: rdm=2, sgt=0, evt[0]=0x20, [1]=0x20, [2]=0x0, nrg=0
nsevreg: registering for 0x20
nsrah: reading (asynchronously) from transport...
nsrah: ...into overflow area...
ntnrd: failed to read 8208 bytes
ntn2err: entry
ntn2err: error: handle=396, op=5, nt[0]=524, nt[1]=997
```

4. **Format Trace File with the *trcasst* utility. Oracle9i Release 2 introduces the Oracle Net Trace assistant to help administrators decipher information contained in the trace files.** The *trcasst* command can be used to provide a more readable trace. This is very helpful when advanced diagnosis is required for problem debugging.

The *trcasst* utility provides the following command line options:

- ***-o*** – Displays services and TTC (Two Task Common) information. Valid options to use with *–o* include:
    - ***c*** – Summary of connection information.
    - ***d*** – Detailed connection information.
    - ***u*** – Summary of TTC information.
    - ***t*** – Detailed TTC information.
    - ***q*** – SQL commands (used in combination with u).

- ***-e*** – Displays error information. Valid options to use with *–e* include:
  - ***0*** – translates NS error numbers.
  - ***1*** – Displays only error translation.
  - ***2*** – Displays error numbers without translation.
- ***-l*** – Displays services and TTC information. Valid options to use with *–l* include:
  - ***a*** – Displays data for all connections in trace file.
  - ***i*** – Displays the trace data for a particular ID from the *–l*a option.
- ***-s*** – Displays a summary of statistics. This includes total bytes sent and received, maximum open cursors, total calls, parse counts, and more.

If no options are specified on the command line, the default will be:

```
trcasst -odt -e0 -s <filename>
```

Sample output generated by the *trcasst* utility is below.

```
C:\oracle9i\network\trace>trcasst listener.trc

Trace Assistant Utility: Version 9.2.0.1.0 Production on February 6, 2003 9:12:
2 PM

(c) Copyright 2002 Oracle Corporation.  All rights reserved.

    **************************************************************************
    *                         Trace Assistant                                *
    **************************************************************************

///////////////////////////////////////////////////////////////
Error found. Error Stack follows:
              id:6
  Operation code:68
      NS Error 1:12537
      NS Error 2:12560
NT Generic Error:507
  Protocol Error:109
        OS Error:0
 NS & NT Errors Translation
12537, 00000 "TNS:connection closed"
 // *Cause: "End of file" condition has been reached; partner has disconnected.

 // *Action: None needed; this is an information message.
/
12560, 00000 "TNS:protocol adapter error"
 // *Cause: A generic protocol adapter error occurred.
 // *Action: Check addresses used for proper protocol specification. Before
 // reporting this error, look at the error stack and check for lower level
 // transport errors.For further details, turn on tracing and reexecute the
 // operation. Turn off tracing when the operation is complete.
/
00507, 00000 "Connection closed"
 // *Cause: Normal "end of file" condition has been reached; partner has
 // disconnected.
 // *Action: None needed; this is an information message.
/
///////////////////////////////////////////////////////////////


----------------------
Trace File Statistics:
----------------------
Total number of Sessions: 0

DATABASE:
  Operation Count:    0 OPENS,     0 PARSES,     0 EXECUTES,     0 FETCHES


ORACLE NET SERVICES:
  Total Calls  :         0 sent,          0 received,          0 oci
  Total Bytes  :         0 sent,          0 received
    Average Bytes:  sent per packet,   received per packet
    Maximum Bytes:          0 sent,          0 received

  Grand Total Packets:      0  sent,       0 received

    **************************************************************************
    *                     Trace Assistant has completed                      *
    **************************************************************************
```

The raw trace file is not nearly as helpful as the results from the *trcasst* utility.

Due to the resources required, tracing the listener activity should be reserved only for debugging connectivity problems. The amount of trace information generated by the tool can be enormous.

Tracking Network Paths and Performance

The Oracle *trcroute* utility (UNIX only) enables DBAs to identify the actual route a connection takes from the client to the server through the Oracle network. *trcroute* will provide very specific error messages in the event of a problem. This makes debugging the connectivity issues much easier. The utility requires an entry from *tnsnames.ora* file on the command line:

```
$ trcroute GRACELANV8_GRA901m

Trace Route Utility for Solaris: Version 9.0.1.0.0 - Production on
03-FEB-2003 1
4:04:51

Copyright (c) 1999 Oracle Corporation.  All rights reserved.

Route of TrcRoute:
------------------

Node: Client           Time and address of entry into node:
-------------------------------------------------------------
03-FEB-2003 14:04:51 ADDRESS= PROTOCOL=TCP  HOST=gracelan
PORT=1525

Node: Server           Time and address of entry into node:
-------------------------------------------------------------
03-FEB-2003 14:04:51 ADDRESS= PROTOCOL=TCP  HOST=gracelan
PORT=1525
```

This example shows the client to server communication route between two listener processes.

Unlike *tnsping*, *trcroute* stops at each network "hop" and gathers certain information before advancing toward the final destination. The listener handles all of the communication with *trcroute,* leaving the database out of the picture.

UNIX provides a utility that will show similar connectivity information between two hosts, independent of any Oracle services. The *traceroute* utility can be found in */usr/sbin* and only requires a host name or IP address.

```
oracle@asgard:/usr/sbin > traceroute gracelan
traceroute to gracelan.bmc.com (172.18.16.215), 30 hops max, 40
byte packets
 1  aus6509vlan2-1.bmc.com (198.64.245.253)  0.431 ms  0.272 ms
0.257 ms
 2  gracelan.bmc.com (172.18.16.215)  0.430 ms  0.400 ms  0.641 ms
```

The result of the *traceroute* command displays the time spent at each stop along the way.

trcroute and *traceroute* are only available on UNIX platforms. If the DBA needs to track the network paths that begin from Windows client machines trying to access a remote database server, the *tracert* utility (trace route) can be used. *tracert* has nothing to do with the listener, but it does indicate the number of hops required to get from point A to point B, which can also be very helpful when debugging network connectivity issues.

```
D:\oracle\ora81\bin>tracert www.oracle.com

Tracing route to bigip-www.us.oracle.com [148.87.9.44]
over a maximum of 30 hops:

  1    <10 ms   <10 ms   <10 ms  gate18.bmc.com [172.18.1.63]
  2     *        *        *      Request timed out.
  3     10 ms   <10 ms   <10 ms  192.168.44.2
  4    <10 ms   <10 ms    10 ms  208.241.47.161
  5    <10 ms    10 ms    10 ms  244.ATM1-0.GW1.AUS3.ALTER.NET
[157.130.135.193]
```

```
  6    10 ms    10 ms    30 ms  161.at-6-0-0.XR2.DFW9.ALTER.NET
[152.63.101.86]
  7    40 ms    30 ms    30 ms  0.so-2-0-0.XL2.DFW9.ALTER.NET
[152.63.102.5]
  8   120 ms   160 ms   110 ms  0.so-7-0-0.BR6.DFW9.ALTER.NET
[152.63.103.78]
  9   110 ms    70 ms    80 ms  so-1-0-0.edge1.Dallas1.Level3.net
[209.245.240.141]
 10   271 ms   200 ms   200 ms  so-5-0-0.gar1.Dallas1.level3.net
[209.244.15.161]
 11   321 ms    20 ms    20 ms  unknown.Level3.net [64.159.3.193]
 12   190 ms   220 ms   151 ms  so-3-0-0.mp2.SanJose1.Level3.net
[64.159.1.130]
 13   161 ms   130 ms   160 ms  gige9-
0.hsipaccess1.SanJose1.Level3.net
[64.159.2.39]
 14    50 ms    80 ms    90 ms  unknown.Level3.net [209.245.144.66]
 15   121 ms    60 ms    70 ms  whq4op3o33-swi-1-rtr-1-
v10.us.oracle.com
[148.87.1.6]
 16   200 ms   240 ms   251 ms  bigip-www.us.oracle.com
[148.87.9.44]

Trace complete.
```

The route from this workstation to www.oracle.com took 16 hops. It is easy to see which hops are the longest and where the bottlenecks occur. The number of hops indicates the number of times data is forwarded in the route between the client and the remote host. The more hops, the more time it takes and the greater the chance an error could occur. Although this example uses a remote address (www.oracle.com), a utility such as this can be just as useful when debugging internal network performance.

Third party tools, as pictured in Figure 7.2, display routing information in a graphical format. Tools such as these can make debugging connectivity problems easier and more intuitive.

Hop	%Loss	IP Address	Node Name	Location	Tzone	ms	Graph	Network
0		172.18.64.187	DMOORE.bmc.com	...			0 531	(private use)
1	100							
2		192.168.44.2	-	...		0		(private use)
3		208.241.47.161	-	Ashburn VA 20147		0		UUNET Technologies, In
4		157.130.135.193	244.ATM1-0.GW1.AUS3.ALTER.NET	Austin, TX, USA		62		UUNET Technologies, In
5		152.63.101.86	161.at-6-0-0.XR2.DFW9.ALTER.NE	Dallas, TX, USA		82		UUNET Technologies, In
6		152.63.102.5	0.so-2-0-0.XL2.DFW9.ALTER.NET	Dallas, TX, USA		74		UUNET Technologies, In
7		152.63.103.78	0.so-7-0-0.BR6.DFW9.ALTER.NET	Dallas, TX, USA		11		UUNET Technologies, In
8		209.245.240.141	so-1-0-0.edge1.Dallas1.Level3.net	Dallas, TX, USA		12		Level 3 Communications
9		209.244.15.161	so-5-0-0.gar1.Dallas1.level3.net	Dallas, TX, USA		67		Level 3 Communications
10		64.159.3.186	so-0-0-0.gar2.Dallas1.level3.net	Dallas, TX, USA		19		Level 3 Communications
11		64.159.3.193	unknown.Level3.net	-		74		Level 3 Communications
12		64.159.1.130	so-3-0-0.mp2.SanJose1.Level3.net	San Jose, CA, USA	-08:0(	58		Level 3 Communications
13		64.159.2.39	gige9-0.hsipaccess1.SanJose1.Le	San Jose, CA, USA	-08:0(	62		Level 3 Communications
14		209.245.144.66	unknown.Level3.net	-		113		Level 3 Communications
15		148.87.1.6	whq4op3o33-swi-1-rtr-1-v10.us.ora	Redwood Shores CA		125		Oracle Datenbanksystem
16		**148.87.9.44**	www.oracle.com	Redwood Shores CA		62		Oracle Datenbanksystem
Roundtrip time to www.oracle.com, average = 62ms, min = 50ms, max = 110ms -- 29-Jan-03 4:02:49 PM								

Figure 7.2 - VisualRoute by Visualware

Summary

This chapter discussed the utilities that aid in diagnosing Oracle database and network connectivity issues. *ping* is used to check the heartbeat of remote hosts, while *tnsping* is used to query remote listeners. *trcroute* will display the network route taken between two listeners, while the UNIX utility *traceroute* will display similar metrics for connectivity between two hosts. *trcroute* can be used to view similar information in Windows systems. In addition, third party tools are available that make interpreting the results of these commands much easier.

The next chapter will focus on those Oracle utilities that are very useful for Oracle Developers.

Chapter 8

Utilities for Oracle Developers

Oracle developers can take advantage of many PL/SQL or Java utilities that exist in *$ORACLE_HOME/bin* or in supplied packages.

These utilities can load, encrypt, tune or debug code objects. This chapter will focus on the utilities that perform these functions, including *wrap*, *dbms_profiler*, *dbms_debug*, *loadjava*, *dropjava* and *loadpsp*.

The first of these utilities to be discussed will be the *wrap* utility that allows PL/SQL developers to encrypt their code.

PL/SQL Wrap Utility for Encryption

The wrap utility (*wrap.exe*) provides a way for PL/SQL developers to protect their intellectual property by making their PL/SQL code unreadable. These encryption options have long been available for other programming languages and were introduced for PL/SQL in version 7. It still amazes me at the number of proprietary procedures and packages that are installed in a readable format – plain PL/SQL.

Unfortunately there is no such command as:

```
ALTER PACKAGE BODY [name] WRAP;
```

Instead, the *wrap* utility takes a readable, ASCII text file as input and converts it to a file containing byte code. The result is that the DBA, developers or anyone with database access cannot view the source code in any readable format.

The command line options for *wrap* are:

```
wrap iname=[file] oname=[file]
```

- ***iname*** – The name of the unencrypted PL/SQL file to be used as input (your source file).

- ***oname*** – The name of the output file. This file will be encrypted.

Below is a sample procedure that increases an employee's salary by 15%, if they scored a 5 in their performance rating:

```
create or replace procedure give_raise
    (emp_id in employee.id%type,
     emp_rating  in NUMBER )
   IS
   BEGIN
      -- raises are only given to those that scored a 5
      -- in their rating
    if emp_rating = 5 then
      update employee
      set salary = salary + (salary * .15)
      where id = emp_id;
    end if;
   END ;
```

Once added to the dictionary, the data dictionary views display the source code for this procedural object:

```
SQL> select text from user_source where name = 'GIVE_RAISE';

TEXT
------------------------------------------------------------
procedure give_raise
    (emp_id in employee.id%type,
     emp_rating  in NUMBER )
   IS
   BEGIN
      -- raises are only given to those that scored a 5
      -- in their rating
    if emp_rating = 5 then
      update employee
      set salary = salary + (salary * .15)
      where id = emp_id;
    end if;
   END ;

13 rows selected.
```

Any user that has been granted the DBA privilege can see the contents of the procedure (*dba_source*), including in this case, the company formula for raises. To prevent this, the stored procedure needs to be wrapped and replaced in the database.

```
C:\oracle9i\bin>wrap iname=giveraise.sql
oname=give_raise_encrypted.sql

PL/SQL Wrapper: Release 9.2.0.1.0- Production on Sun Dec 08
14:28:41 2002

Copyright (c) Oracle Corporation 1993, 2001.  All Rights Reserved.

Processing giveraise.sql to give_raise_encrypted.sql
```

Once wrapped, the procedure can be resubmitted to the database:

```
SQL> @c:\oracle9i\bin\give_raise_encrypted.sql

Procedure Created.
```

Now, another query against *user_source* shows the newly wrapped code:

```
SQL> select text from user_source where name = 'GIVE_RAISE';

TEXT
-----------------------------------------------------------
procedure give_raise wrapped
0
abcd
abcd
abcd
abcd
abcd
abcd
abcd
abcd
abcd
0 9a 8f :2 a0 6b :2 a0 f b0
3d 8f a0 b0 3d b4 55 6a
a0 7e 51 b4 2e :3 a0 7e 51
b4 2e e7 :2 a0 7e b4 2e ef
f9 e9 b7 19 3c b7 a4 b1
11 68 4f 1d 17 b5
 ...
```

Notice the output of the query above appears like garbage, or at least not readable code. Nothing except *Oracle.exe* can now read the logic for generating raises.

Best Practices for Using Wrap

- **Always wrap code that contains sensitive information or commercial software that is owned and distributed by your company.** The *give_raise* procedure is highly sensitive and should not reveal the code to anyone that can access a DBA view.

- **Although the *wrap* utility does in fact work in a straightforward manner, it will not work when wrapping code that is specific to a version of the database.** For instance, our example above would wrap fine in version 7, and the same encrypted output can be used in 9i. But, if the code contains PL/SQL commands specific to a version of the database (*execute immediate*), then the wrap executable must be at least at that level of the database.

- **Wrapping a procedure in 9i will not compile when submitted to an Oracle7 database.** For the same reason that a file created in Word/XP cannot be loaded into Word95, newer versions of *wrap* only work with that version of the database. The wrap utility does have a "loose" connection to the database, although it does not ask for one (username, password, SID). Attempting to wrap code that will not compile, will result in errors like the one below:

```
C:\oracle9i\bin>wrap iname=giveraise.sql oname=giveraise.wrp

PL/SQL Wrapper: Release 9.2.0.1.0- Production on Sun Dec 08 15:42:23 2002

Copyright (c) Oracle Corporation 1993, 2001.  All Rights Reserved.

Processing giveraise.sql to giveraise.wrp
PSU(103,1,8,1):Encountered the symbol "IF" when expecting one of the following:

   constant exception <an identifier>
   <a double-quoted delimited-identifier> table LONG_ double ref
   char time timestamp interval date binary national character
   nchar

PL/SQL Wrapper error: Compilation error(s) for:
create or replace procedure give_raise
Outputting source and continuing.
```

It would seem to make sense to just *wrap* all code with the oldest version of the wrap utility, but that will not work. For example, trying to wrap a procedure that contained a version specific command (like *execute immediate*) would require that specific version of the wrap executable. In fact, it is much easier to wrap a file on each version of the database that you plan to support. Also, code that is wrapped is portable to any platform. Therefore, PL/SQL code could be wrapped on Windows and distributed to any UNIX platform.

- Give careful consideration to wrapping code since it increases the size of the procedural object (function, procedure, and package) by as much as 200-250%. The size of the wrapped object is the only down side to wrapping; the execution benchmarks are the same.

- Do not wrap package specifications (headers), since they serve as great documentation. Good development practice is to only wrap the implementation, the package body.

- Provide a version of the wrap utility for developers to use. Since *$ORACLE_HOME/bin* is usually very restricted, copy the wrap executable to a shared drive that everyone can use.

No utility exists that will unwrap a wrapped package; otherwise, the wrap utility would be useless.

Now that encryption is addressed, the next step for a developer would be to ensure that the code performs well. Developers can use the *dbms_profiler* utility described in the next section to gain code execution benchmarks.

The dbms_profiler Utility

PL/SQL developers are always trying to optimize their code to perform more efficiently. As of Oracle 8.1.5, a utility exists that assists developers with this process. The *dbms_profiler* is one of the most under-utilized utilities within Oracle.

The basic idea behind profiling is for the developer to understand where their code is spending the most time, so they can detect and optimize it. The profiling utility allows Oracle to collect data in memory structures and then dumps it into tables as application code is executed. *dbms_profiler* is to PL/SQL, what *tkprof* and Explain Plan are to SQL.

Installation

The profiling tools are not a part of the base installation of Oracle, so that will require more on the part of the developer. Two tables need to be installed along with the Oracle supplied PL/SQL package.

In the *$ORACLE_HOME/rdbms/admin* directory, two files exist that create the environment needed for the profiler to execute.

- ***proftab.sql*** - Creates three tables and a sequence and must be executed before the *profload.sql* file.

- ***profload.sql*** - Creates the package header and package body for DBMS_PROFILER. This script must be executed as the SYS user.

Once the environment is established, the three tables created by *proftab.sql* contain the vital information needed to benchmark PL/SQL performance. Queries against these tables will provide the insight needed to optimize the PL/SQL code.

The *plsql_profiler_runs* table contains information related to a profiling session. Things, such as when the run was started, who started it, and how long the run lasted are contained in this table. This table has the following important columns:

- ***runid*** - This is the unique run identifier given to each profiler execution.

- ***related_run*** - Runid of related run that can be called by the programmer.

- ***run_owner*** - User who started the run.

- ***run_date*** - Timestamp of the date of the run.

- ***run_comment*** – User provided text concerning anything about this run that they wish to specify. This is used mainly for documentation, since *run_id* is hard to remember.

- **run_total_time** – Total elapsed time for this run.

The *plsql_profiler_units* table defines each PL/SQL component (unit) that was executed during a profiler run. Benchmarks for each of the units are stored in this table in the following columns:

- ***runid*** - References *plsql_profiler_runs*(runid).
- ***unit_number*** - Internally generated library unit number.
- ***unit_type*** - Library unit type (PACKAGE, PROCEDURE, etc).
- ***unit_owner*** - Library unit owner name (the owner of the object).
- ***unit_name*** - Library unit name (the name of the object as defined in the *user_objects* view).
- ***unit_timestamp*** – Time when the unit was created. The "unit", being the procedural object (procedure, function, package). This column holds the same data as the created column in the *user_objects* view.
- ***total_time*** – Total time used by this unit for the given run.

The primary key for this table is *runid*, *unit_number.*

The *plsql_profiler_data* table is where the real performance benchmarks are stored. This table contains the execution statistics for each line of code contained in our PL/SQL unit. This table can be joined to the *user_source* view and can extract the actual line of code for each benchmark. The primary key includes *runid*, *unit_number*, and *line#*.

The *plsql_profiler_data* table has the following important columns as indicated by the results of the following query:

```
select runid, unit_number, line#, total_occur, total_time,
       min_time, max_time
from plsql_profiler_data;
```

RUNID	UNIT_NUMBER	LINE#	TOTAL_OCCUR	TOTAL_TIME	MIN_TIME	MAX_TIME
1	1	8	3	33284677	539733	28918759
1	1	80	2	1134222	516266	617955
1	1	89	0	0	0	0
1	1	90	0	0	0	0
1	1	92	0	0	0	0
1	1	95	0	0	0	0
1	1	103	0	0	0	0
1	1	111	0	0	0	0
1	1	112	0	0	0	0
1	1	116	1	1441523	1441523	1441523
1	1	119	0	0	0	0
1	1	121	1	1431466	1431466	1431466
1	1	123	1	136330	136330	136330
1	1	132	1	978895	978895	978895
1	1	140	0	0	0	0
1	1	141	0	0	0	0
1	1	143	0	0	0	0
1	1	146	1	2905397	2905397	2905397
1	1	152	2	1622552	574374	1048177
1	1	153	0	0	0	0
1	1	157	1	204495	204495	204495
1	1	160	0	0	0	0

The *line#* above is used to tie these execution benchmarks back to a line of source in the *user_source* view.

The *profload.sql* file contains calls to two other files:

- ***dbmspbp.sql*** – This file creates the actual *sys.dbms_profiler* package. This must be created as the SYS user, which is the main drawback of this utility.

- ***prvtpbp.plb*** – This file creates the *sys.dbms_profiler_lib* library object and it is wrapped. Again, this must be executed as the SYS user.

Figure 8.1 depicts the relationships between the three profiler tables, as well as the indirect relationship to the *dba_source* or *user_source* view (Source). Note that everything begins with a RUN and drills down to the real performance data for a particular PL/SQL line of code.

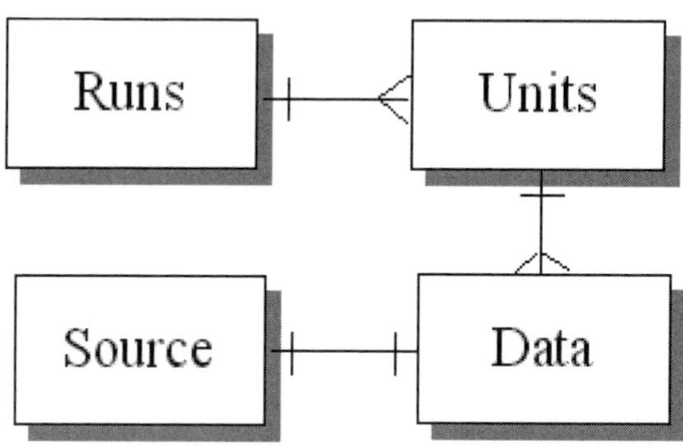

Figure 8.1 – Relationships between dbms_profiler tables

The environment is now configured, and the profiling utility is ready to be put to work.

Starting a Profiling Session

The profiler does not begin capturing performance information until the call to *start_profiler* is executed.

```
SQL> exec dbms_profiler.start_profiler('Test of raise procedure by
Scott');

PL/SQL procedure successfully completed.
```

The profiler captures data on a session-by-session basis. This means that if the user SCOTT started the profiler by executing the command above, only PL/SQL objects that were executed and owned by SCOTT will be profiled, and consequently have data in the profiler tables described earlier. The SCOTT user is only used as an example; it could be any database user.

Flushing Data during a Profiling Session

The flush command enables the developer to dump statistics during program execution without stopping the profiling utility. The only other time Oracle saves data to the underlying tables is when the profiling session is stopped, as shown below:

```
SQL> exec dbms_profiler.flush_data();

PL/SQL procedure successfully completed.
```

A developer could use the *flush* procedure with *dbms_debug* and step, line by line, through a procedure, flushing performance benchmarks along the way. Or, if you have a very long running

PL/SQL program, flushing data can be very useful in the performance tuning process.

Stopping a Profiling Session

Stopping a profiler execution is done after an adequate period of time of gathering performance benchmarks – determined by the developer. Once the developer stops the profiler, all the remaining (unflushed) data is loaded into the profiler tables.

```
SQL> exec dbms_profiler.stop_profiler();

PL/SQL procedure successfully completed.
```

The *dbms_profiler* package also provides procedures that suspend and resume profiling (*pause_profiler()*, *resume_profiler()*).

Now that the profiler has stopped, the data is available for diagnostics from within Oracle, and we can begin working with it.

Working with Captured Profiler Data

The profiler utility populates three tables with information, *plsql_profiler_runs*, *plsql_profiler_units*, and *plsql_profiler_data*. Each "run" is initiated by a user and contains zero or more "units". Each unit contains "data" about its execution – the guts of the performance data benchmarks.

The performance information for a line in a unit needs to be tied back to the line source in *user_source*. Once that join is made, the developer will have all of the information that they need to optimize, enhance, and tune their application code, as well as the SQL.

Useful Scripts

To extract high-level data, including the length of a particular run, the script (*profiler_runs.sql*) below can be executed:

profiler_runs.sql

```
column runid format 990
column type format a15
column run_comment format a20
column object_name format a20

select a.runid,
     substr(b.run_comment, 1, 20) as run_comment,
     decode(a.unit_name, '', '<anonymous>',
          substr(a.unit_name,1, 20)) as object_name,
     TO_CHAR(a.total_time/1000000000, '99999.99') as sec,
     TO_CHAR(100*a.total_time/b.run_total_time, '999.9') as pct
     from plsql_profiler_units a, plsql_profiler_runs b
     where a.runid=b.runid
     order by a.runid asc;
```

```
RUNID UNIT_NUMBER OBJECT_NAME          TYPE            SEC       PCT
----- ----------- -------------------- --------------- --------- ------
    1           1 <anonymous>                                .00     .0
    1           2 <anonymous>                               1.01     .0
    1           3 BMC$PKKPKG           PACKAGE BODY      6921.55   18.2
    1           4 <anonymous>                                .02     .0
    2           1 <anonymous>                                .00     .0
    2           2 <anonymous>                                .01     .0

6 rows selected.
```

Note that anonymous PL/SQL blocks are also included in the profiler tables. Anonymous blocks are less useful from a tuning perspective since they cannot be tied back to a source object in *user_source*. Anonymous PL/SQL blocks are simply runtime source objects and do not have a corresponding dictionary object (*package, procedure, function*). For this reason, the anonymous blocks should be eliminated from most reports.

From the data displayed above, the next step is to focus on the lines within the package body, *testproc*, that are taking the longest. The script (*profiler_top10_lines.sql*) below displays the line numbers and their performance benchmarks of the top 10 worst performing lines of code.

profiler_top10_lines.sql

```
select line#, total_occur,
  decode (total_occur,null,0,0,0,total_time/total_occur/1000,0) as
avg,
  decode(total_time,null,0,total_time/1000) as total_time,
  decode(min_time,null,0,min_time/1000) as min,
  decode(max_time,null,0,max_time/1000) as max
  from plsql_profiler_data
  where runid = 1
  and unit_number = 3          -- testproc
  and rownum < 11              -- only show Top 10
  order by total_time desc ;
```

```
     LINE# TOTAL_OCCUR        AVG TOTAL_TIME        MIN        MAX
---------- ----------- ---------- ---------- ---------- ----------
       156           1              5008.457   5008.457   5008.457
        27           1               721.879    721.879    721.879
      2113           1               282.717    282.717    282.717
        89           1               138.565    138.565    138.565
      2002           1               112.863    112.863    112.863
      1233           1                94.984     94.984     94.984
        61           1                94.984     94.984     94.984
       866           1                94.984     94.984     94.984
       481           1                92.749     92.749     92.749
       990           1                90.514     90.514     90.514

10 rows selected.
```

Taking it one step further, the query below (*profiler_line_source.sql*) will extract the actual source code for the top 10 worst performing lines.

 **profiler_line_source.sql**

```
select line#,
 decode (a.total_occur,null,0,0,0,
 a.total_time/a.total_occur/1000) as Avg,
 substr(c.text,1,20) as Source
 from plsql_profiler_data a, plsql_profiler_units b, user_source c
    where a.runid          = 1
    and a.unit_number      = 3
    and a.runid            = b.runid
    and a.unit_number      = b.unit_number
    and b.unit_name        = c.name
    and a.line#            = c.line
    and rownum             < 11
    order by a.total_time desc ;
```

```
     LINE#        AVG SOURCE
---------- ---------- --------------------
       156   5008.457   select sum(bytes) into reusable_var from dba_free_space;
        27    721.879   execute immediate dml_str USING  current_time
      2113    282.717   select OBJ#, TYPE# from SYS.OBJ$;
        89    138.565   OBJ_TYPES(BOBJ(I)) := BTYP(I);
      2002    112.863   select count(*) into reusable_var from dba_objects
      1233     94.984   delete from pkk_daily_activity
        61     94.984   update_stats_table(33, reusable_var, null);
       866     94.984   latest_executions := reusable_var - total_executions;
       481     92.749   time_number := hours + round(minutes * 100/60/100,2);
       990     90.514   update_stats_table(45, LOBS, null);

10 rows selected.
```

Notice from the output above that most of the information needed to diagnose and fix PL/SQL performance issues is provided. For lines containing SQL statements, the tuner can optimize the SQL perhaps by adding optimizer hints, eliminating full table scans, etc. Consult Chapter 5 for more details on using *tkprof* utility to diagnose SQL issues.

Other useful scripts that are hidden within the Oracle directory structure (*$ORACLE_HOME/PLSQL/DEMO*) include a few gems that help report and analyze profiler information.

- ***profdemo.sql*** -A demo script for collecting PL/SQL profiler data.

- ***profsum.sql*** - A collection of useful SQL scripts that are executed against profiler tables.

- ***profrep.sql*** – Creates views and a package (unwrapped) that populates the views based on the three underlying profiler tables.

Best Practices for Using *dbms_profiler* Everywhere

- **Wrap only for production** - Wrapping code is desired for production environments but not for profiling. It is much easier to see the unencrypted form of the text in our reports than it is to connect line numbers to source versions. Use *dbms_profiler* before you wrap your code in a test environment, wrap it, and then put it in production.

- **Eliminate system packages most of the time** - Knowing the performance data for internal Oracle processing does not buy you much since you cannot change anything. However, knowing the performance problem is within the system packages will save you some tuning time since the problem is somewhere other than your own code.

- When analyzing lines of code, it is best to concentrate on the following:

- **Lines of code that are frequently executed** - For example, a loop that executes 5000 times is a great candidate for tuning. Guru Oracle tuners typically look for that "low hanging fruit" in which one line or a group of lines of code are executed much more than others. The benefits of tuning one line of code that is executed often far outweigh tuning those lines that may cost more yet are executed infrequently in comparison.

- **Lines of code with a high value for average time executed** – The minimum and maximum values of execution time are interesting although not as useful as the average execution time. Min and max only tell us how much the execution time varies depending on database activity. Line by line, a PL/SQL developer should focus on those lines that cost the most on an average execution basis. *dbms_profiler* does not provide the average, but it does provide enough data to allow it to be computed (Total Execution Time / # Times Executed).

- **Lines of code that contain SQL syntax** - The main resource consumers are those lines that execute SQL. Once the data is sorted by average execution time, the statements that are the worst usually contain SQL. Optimize and tune the SQL through utilities, such as Explain Plan, *tkprof*, and third party software.

Obtaining execution statistics for PL/SQL code is a requirement for good PL/SQL developers. The next section describes how developers can fully debug their code, stepping line by line through PL/SQL code during execution by utilizing the *dbms_debug* utility.

The *dbms_debug* Utility

Oracle ships with the *dbms_debug* package, which is another useful programming utility for PL/SQL Developers. These programmers, when working in other languages, such as C, C++, and Java utilize an Integrated Development Environment (IDE) to peek into the runtime execution of the code by offering the following features:

- Setting breakpoints
- Inspecting variable contents
- Pause and terminate execution

Complete IDE functionality is outside the scope of this book since there are many PL/SQL IDEs on the market. The important thing to know is that they all use the *dbms_debug* package provided by Oracle, which is what this section explains. Without it, developers usually end up modifying the code to write values to temporary tables or to the screen during execution. This involves creating many lines of debugging code instead of using the debug facility.

The debug facility requires two sessions: the first session is used for execution of the code being debugged. Oracle refers to this session as the "target" session. The second session is the one that submits the debug commands, and for that reason, the second session is termed the "debug" session.

From the target session, a function will be created and compiled for debug.

Initializing a Debug Session

In the target session, the following function, listed below, will be created. This function does nothing more than loop for the amount specified in the function call. This function is only used as an example of something that can be debugged. In the examples below, the SQL prompt is changed to reflect the session to which it applies: SQL-TARGET or SQL-DEBUG.

```
SQL-TARGET>  create or replace function loop_tester(ctr number)
return number
       is
         ret number:=0;
       begin
         for i in 1..ctr loop
           ret := ret + 1;
         end loop;
         return ret;
      end;
   /

Function created.

SQL-TARGET> alter function loop_tester compile debug;
```

```
Function altered.

SQL-TARGET> select dbms_debug.initialize from dual;

INITIALIZE
---------------------------------------------
000900DB0001

SQL-TARGET> exec dbms_debug.debug_on;
```

The debug session now will use the *initialize* procedure and return a number to initiate the debug session. Once the number is returned from *initialize*, the *attach_session* procedure will use it to attach from the debug session.

```
SQL-DEBUG> exec dbms_debug.attach_session('000900DB0001');

PL/SQL procedure successfully completed.
```

This function was compiled for debug explicitly. Another option is to establish debug mode for the entire session. This instructs the compiler to generate debug for all PL/SQL in the session and does not require any recomilation.

```
ALTER SESSION SET PLSQL_DEBUG = true;
```

Setting a Breakpoint

The code below, submitted from the debug session, will set a breakpoint on line 6 (ret := ret + 1;) of the function that SCOTT created in the target session.

```
SQL-DEBUG> set serveroutput on
SQL-DEBUG> declare
        info dbms_debug.program_info;
        bnumber binary_integer;
        return_int  binary_integer;
        begin
```

```
       info.namespace :=
dbms_debug.namespace_pkgspec_or_toplevel;
       info.name      := 'LOOP_TESTER';
       info.owner     := 'SCOTT';
       info.dblink    := null;   -- no dblink access
       info.line#     := 6;      -- line we want the break
       return_int:= dbms_debug.set_breakpoint(info,3,bnumber);
       -- check for returned error
       if return_int != dbms_debug.success then
         dbms_output.put_line('Error Setting breakpoint');
       else
         dbms_output.put_line('Breakpoint set!');
       end if;
     end;
 /
Breakpoint set!
```

PL/SQL procedure successfully completed. That is a lot of work just to set a breakpoint! Most Oracle developers that utilize the *dbms_debug* package usually create a wrapper package of their own that makes it easier to use directly from the SQL*Plus prompt without requiring anonymous PL/SQL blocks. This package would be created once by the developer and used repeatedly instead of accessing *dbms_debug* directly through anonymous PL/SQL calls, as in the example above.

Synchronizing

Synchronization is the process of the debug session waiting for the target session to execute and hit a breakpoint. The following code will be executed from the debug session and will hang until a breakpoint occurs.

```
SQL-DEBUG>  DECLARE
     runinfo    dbms_debug.runtime_info;
     retval     binary_integer;
     BEGIN
        retval := dbms_debug.synchronize(runinfo, 0 +
                    dbms_debug.info_getstackdepth +
                    dbms_debug.info_getbreakpoint +
                    dbms_debug.info_getlineinfo + 0);
```

```
      if retval = dbms_debug.success then
         dbms_output.put_line(' Sync Successful ');
      else
         dbms_output.put_line(' Sync Unsuccessful error = '
                              || retval);
      end if;
    END;
/
Sync Successful
```

The next step is to call the function and debug the code. The statement below will execute the *loop_tester* function and cause the breakpoint to be hit:

```
SQL-TARGET> select loop_tester(500) from dual;
```

Viewing and Modifying Variables

Once the breakpoint is hit, the debug facility pauses execution of the program. The power of any debugger is in its ability to inspect and change variable values at runtime. The code below will get the value of the "*ctr*" variable and display it in SQL*Plus:

```
SQL-DEBUG> DECLARE
    frame      number;
    varvalue   VARCHAR2(500);
    retval     binary_integer;
    varname    varchar2(32);
    BEGIN
      varname := 'CTR';
      frame   := 0 ;
      retval  := dbms_debug.get_value(varname, frame, varvalue,
NULL);
      dbms_output.put_line('The value of the variable ' ||
varname ||
             ' is ' || varvalue);
    END;
/

The value of the variable CTR is 500

PL/SQL procedure successfully completed.
```

So far, everything looks correct. A value of 500 was passed to the function, and the value returned by the *get_value* procedure was the same. Next, the *set_value* procedure will be executed in order to change the value to 700:

```
SQL-DEBUG> DECLARE
     frame      number;
     retval     binary_integer;
     BEGIN
        frame := 0;
        retval := dbms_debug.set_value (frame, 'ctr := 700;');
        if retval = dbms_debug.success then
           dbms_output.put_line('Variable change successful');
        else
           dbms_output.put_line('Variable change unsuccessful');
        end if;
     END;
  /

Variable change successful
```

The variable "*ctr*" is once again retrieved via *get_value*, and the output reveals that the new value has been loaded into the program.

```
SQL> DECLARE
     frame      number;
     varvalue   VARCHAR2(500);
     retval     binary_integer;
     varname    varchar2(32);
     BEGIN
       varname := 'CTR';
       frame   := 0 ;
       retval  := dbms_debug.get_value(varname, frame, varvalue,
NULL);
       dbms_output.put_line('The value of the variable ' ||
varname ||
                ' is ' || varvalue);
     END;
  /

The value of the variable CTR is 700

PL/SQL procedure successfully completed.
```

The developer can then choose to continue execution (*dbms_debug.continue*), add more breakpoints, delete breakpoints, or whatever is needed to analyze the issues with the code.

The ability to inspect and modify variable values at runtime is a prerequisite for any development environment. It allows developers to test code during the actual execution without writing additional code for the sole purpose of testing.

Many procedures exist within the *dbms_debug* package. A developer can utilize these to create a complete debug environment, set break points, inspect variable values, pause program execution, etc. When errors occur during debugging, one way to map the error numbers to messages is to view the source for *dbms_debug* located in *$ORACLE_HOME/rdbms/admin/dbmspb.sql.*

dbms_debug is a powerful, yet somewhat difficult to use, utility for Oracle developers. It is easy to see why third party tools (Figure 8.2) are successful with products that serve as an API to *dbms_debug*, with a robust user interface and insulation from the details of the utility.

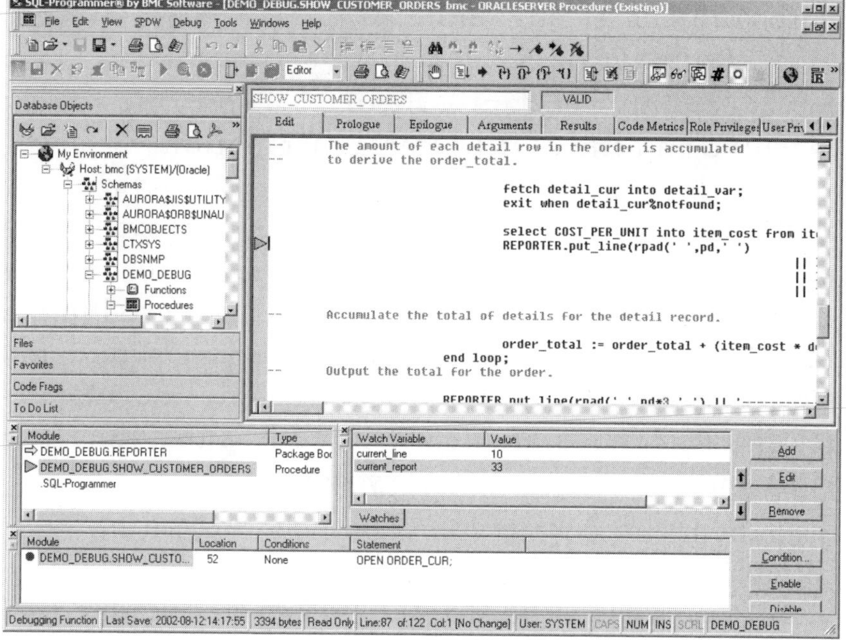

Figure 8.2 – SQL Programmer (Third Party Product)

Developers should leverage this utility for inspecting and changing runtime variables instead of inserting code that writes values to tables. Once mastered, *dbms_debug* is impossible to live without.

The next utility for developers is one that is used by Java programmers to embed SQL statements directly within their Java code – SQLJ.

The SQLJ Utility

The SQLJ Utility (*sqlj.exe*) is for Java developers seeking alternatives to JDBC for Oracle database access. This utility is roughly equivalent to the Pro*C and Pro*COBOL precompilers. Given that entire books are written on SQLJ, this book will detail the use of the SQLJ executable. This example requires a working version of the Java SDK, either version 1.3 or 1.4 on the client machine and the SQLJ Oracle installation.

SQLJ is an industry standard that provides an easier way for Java programmers to access databases via SQL. Without SQLJ, they are limited to JDBC result set processing, an error prone and time-consuming process. SQLJ enables developers to insert SQL statements directly into the Java code indicated by the *#sql* syntax:

```
#sql users = { select username from v$session };
```

The *sqlj.exe* file is used to convert SQLJ syntax to a Java source file and optionally, a class file that can be executed. And, after viewing the messy generated Java source file, it is easy to see the value of SQLJ. This is not a Java source that someone would want to maintain.

The following *.sqlj* file (*Util_Sessions.sqlj*) will be used as an example. This SQLJ source simply queries the database for the names of the users connected and displays them.

Util_Sessions.sqlj

```
package com.rampant.sqljexample;

import java.sql.SQLException;
import oracle.sqlj.runtime.Oracle;

public class CurrentSessions {

   #sql static public iterator userIterator(String username);

   public static void main (String args[]) {
   try {
      Oracle.connect("jdbc:oracle:oci8:@ORCL92", "scott", "tiger");

      userIterator users = null;

      // retrieve the data into the iterator
      #sql users = { select username from v$session };

      while (users.next()) {
          System.out.println(users.username());
      }
   }

   catch (SQLException se) {
      System.out.println("Error " + se.toString());
   }

   finally {
      try {
         Oracle.close();
      }
      catch (SQLException sqle) {
         System.out.println("Cannot close connection");
      }
   }
}
```

At the operating system level, the Java environment must be configured. The following DOS commands ensure that *JAVA_HOME* is set and also appends the three zip files below to the CLASSPATH. These zip files are needed for the SQLJ executable to perform.

```
C:\oracle9i\bin>echo %JAVA_HOME%
c:\j2sdk1.4.0_01

C:\oracle9i\bin>SET
CLASSPATH=%CLASSPATH%;%ORACLE_HOME%\sqlj\lib\translator.zip
```

```
C:\oracle9i\bin>SET
CLASSPATH=%CLASSPATH%;%ORACLE_HOME%\sqlj\lib\runtime12.zip

C:\oracle9i\bin>SET
CLASSPATH=%CLASSPATH%;%ORACLE_HOME%\jdbc\lib\classes12.zip

C:\oracle9i\bin>sqlj -compile=true -user=scott/tiger -status -
ser2class -warn CurrentSessions.sqlj

[Translating]
[Reading file CurrentSessions]
[Translating file CurrentSessions]
[Compiling]
```

Here is the resulting Java file (*CurrentSessions.java*) as generated by the *sqlj.exe*. The SQLJ executable created a corresponding Java file that will be compiled and executed as part of our program. The SQLJ file is used only for the purpose of generating the Java file.

CurrentSessions.java

```
/*@lineinfo:filename=CurrentSessions*//*@lineinfo:user-
code*//*@lineinfo:1^1*/package com.rampant.sqljexample;

import java.sql.SQLException;
import oracle.sqlj.runtime.Oracle;

public class CurrentSessions {

   /*@lineinfo:generated-code*//*@lineinfo:8^4*/

//  ***********************************************************
//  SQLJ iterator declaration:
//  ***********************************************************

public static class userIterator
extends sqlj.runtime.ref.ResultSetIterImpl
implements sqlj.runtime.NamedIterator
{
  public userIterator(sqlj.runtime.profile.RTResultSet resultSet)
    throws java.sql.SQLException
  {
    super(resultSet);
    usernameNdx = findColumn("username");
    m_rs = (oracle.jdbc.OracleResultSet)
resultSet.getJDBCResultSet();
  }
  private oracle.jdbc.OracleResultSet m_rs;
  public String username()
    throws java.sql.SQLException
```

```
    {
      return m_rs.getString(usernameNdx);
    }
    private int usernameNdx;
  }


// ************************************************************
/*@lineinfo:user-code*//*@lineinfo:8^60*/

    public static void main (String args[]) {
    try {
       Oracle.connect("jdbc:oracle:oci8:@ORCL92", "scott", "tiger");

       userIterator users = null;

       // retrieve the data into the iterator
       /*@lineinfo:generated-code*//*@lineinfo:17^7*/

// ************************************************************
//  #sql users = { select username from v$session  };
// ************************************************************

{
  // declare temps
  oracle.jdbc.OraclePreparedStatement __sJT_st = null;
  sqlj.runtime.ref.DefaultContext __sJT_cc =
sqlj.runtime.ref.DefaultContext.getDefaultContext(); if
(__sJT_cc==null)
sqlj.runtime.error.RuntimeRefErrors.raise_NULL_CONN_CTX();
  sqlj.runtime.ExecutionContext.OracleContext __sJT_ec =
((__sJT_cc.getExecutionContext()==null) ?
sqlj.runtime.ExecutionContext.raiseNullExecCtx() :
__sJT_cc.getExecutionContext().getOracleContext());
  try {
   __sJT_st =
__sJT_ec.prepareOracleStatement(__sJT_cc,"0com..sqljexample.Current
Sessions","select username from v$session");
   // execute query
   users = new com..sqljexample.CurrentSessions.userIterator(new
sqlj.runtime.ref.OraRTResultSet(__sJT_ec.oracleExecuteQuery(),__sJT
_st,"0com..sqljexample.CurrentSessions",null));
  } finally { __sJT_ec.oracleCloseQuery(); }
}


// ************************************************************

/*@lineinfo:user-code*//*@lineinfo:17^53*/

      while (users.next()) {
          System.out.println(users.username());
      }
   }

   catch (SQLException se) {
      System.out.println("Error " + se.toString());
   }
```

```
   finally {
      try {
         Oracle.close();
      }
      catch (SQLException sqle) {
         System.out.println("Cannot close connection");
      }
   }

}
}/*@lineinfo:generated-code*/
```

Notice that the SQLJ process inserted some special syntax into the generated Java file. Developers should only maintain the *sqlj* file, however, and not be concerned with editing the *sqlj* generated Java file.

Once *CurrentSessions.java* is compiled into a class file, it can be executed. Notice from the output below that three users are connected to the database. This Java program was executed by simply invoking the entire class name at the operating system command line.

```
C:\oracle9i\bin>java com.rampant.sqljexample.CurrentSessions
 SYSTEM
 SYS
 SCOTT
```

That is a very simple example, but in a few lines of code, a Java program was created that accessed the database and returned a list of connected users.

SQLJ provides the Java developer with an extensive list of command line options. These enable the Java developer to fully control the SQLJ development environment. These options can be viewed by typing *sqlj* at the command line with no additional parameters.

Conclusion

The advantages of SQLJ include:

- **The automatic validation of SQL code.** With JDBC, SQL and DML statements are only validated at runtime and not compile time, since the SQL is only known as a String object to JDBC. SQLJ will not allow invalid SQL to compile and will inform the developer at development time instead of runtime.

- **The readability of the Java code.** SQLJ can accomplish the same tasks as JDBC with much fewer lines. In addition, it is much easier to read SQL and DML statements inline in Java.

The disadvantages to SQLJ include:

- The extra step needed to create compiled code to access the database. An extra step is one more opportunity for problems to occur.

- The readability of the generated Java code.

Whether the developer chooses to use JDBC or SQLJ when writing server-side code, the code still needs to be loaded into the database. The *loadjava* utility is important because it provides this capability directly from the operating system command line.

Loading and Dropping Java Objects

The *loadjava* utility (Oracle 8.1.5 and up) loads Java source and class files into the database. When class files are created in a conventional manner, outside the database, *loadjava* is used to get them into the database.

loadjava requires two database privileges to load java objects into your own schema: CREATE PROCEDURE and CREATE TABLE. To load Java objects into a schema other than the currently connected user, CREATE ANY PROCEDURE and CREATE ANY TABLE privileges are required.

This example will use a simple Java program that will be compiled outside of Oracle and then loaded into the database.

```
public class SimpleJava {

   public void main(String[] args) {
      System.out.println("Here we are");
   }
```

From DOS or UNIX :

```
C:\oracle9i\bin>javac SimpleJava.java

C:\oracle9i\bin>loadjava -user scott/tiger SimpleJava.class
```

The class file is now loaded into the database and visible from the *dba_objects* view with an object type of JAVA CLASS.

From SQL*Plus, create the PL/SQL wrapper to invoke the newly loaded Java class:

```
SQL> create or replace procedure call_simplejava
  2  as language java
  3  name 'SimpleJava.showMessage()';
  4  /
```

Execute the code from SQL*Plus:

```
SQL> set serveroutput on;
SQL> call dbms_java.set_output(50);

Call completed.

SQL> execute call_simplejava;
Here we are

PL/SQL procedure successfully completed.
```

In this example, the Java class file was loaded into the database. The Java source file can also be loaded. But, both the source and class files cannot be loaded at the same time.

```
C:\oracle9i\bin>loadjava -user scott/tiger SimpleJava.java
```

If loading many Java class files at one time, it is advisable to put them in a JAR file and load them into the database at one time, since the *loadjava* program will also load JAR files. A JAR file is a group of Java class files lumped into one file, a format similar to TAR (on UNIX) and WinZip (on Windows). The contents of a JAR file can be viewed using these popular utilities. Java developers prefer to distribute a few JAR files rather than many individual Java class files.

loadjava provides many command line options for the Java developer. The complete list can be viewed by typing *loadjava* at the command line.

Just as *loadjava* loads the database with our Java files or classes, the *dropjava* utility deletes them. In the example below, the class file that was loaded with *loadjava* is removed. And just like *loadjava*, it will drop Java source, Java classes, or JAR files.

```
C:\oracle9i\bin>dropjava -u scott/tiger SimpleJava.class
```

Alternatively, instead of using the command line utility, you can call a package that will do the same thing:

```
SQL> call dbms_java.dropjava('... options...');
```

Dropjava can be used to delete Java objects from the database. These Java objects may have been loaded into the database through the *loadjava* utility. The next utility also loads code into the database; only instead of Java, it loads a PL/SQL Server Page (PSP).

Loading PL/SQL Server Pages

The *loadpsp* utility loads a PSP (PL/SQL Server Page) file from the operating system into the database. The loaded PSP can then be accessed from a URL to display database content on a web page.

PL/SQL Server Pages (PSP) are Oracle's answer to the more common Java Server pages. It provides a convenient way for developers to display database content on web pages. By simply accessing a URL that points to a PSP, the result set of the data is displayed on the web page in the HTML format the developer has specified.

The PL/SQL Web Toolkit ships as part of the database in Oracle 9i. The file below (*Parmlist.psp*) will serve as the example in which the web page will display the parameter names and values from the *v$parameter* table.
This simple PSP accesses the name and value from the *v$paramater* table and formats them in very basic HTML. Additional logic is added to check for null parameter values, in which case null will be displayed.

parmlist.psp

```
<%@ page language="PL/SQL" %>
<%@ plsql procedure="ParmListPSP" %>
<HTML>
<HEAD><TITLE>This is a PSP Page!</TITLE></HEAD>
<BODY>
This is a list of current database parameters: <BR><BR>

<% FOR parm IN (select name, value from v$parameter
                order by name)
LOOP
  if parm.value is null then
     parm.value := 'null';
  end if;
  %>
  <TR>
  <TD><%= parm.name %></TD>
  =
  <TD><%= parm.value %></TD><BR>
  </TR>
<% END LOOP; %>
</BODY>
</HTML>
```

The PSP file can be loaded from the DOS or UNIX prompt using *loadpsp*:

```
C:\oracle9i\bin> loadpsp -replace -user scott/tiger Parmlist.psp
"Parmlist.psp": procedure "ParmListPSP" created.
```

The procedure is now queried from the data dictionary:

```
SQL> select text from user_source where name = 'PARMLISTPSP' order
by line;

TEXT
------------------------------------------------------------------
PROCEDURE ParmListPSP  AS
 BEGIN NULL;
htp.prn('
');
htp.prn('
<HTML>
<HEAD><TITLE>This is a PSP Page!</TITLE></HEAD>
<BODY>
This is a list of current database parameters: <BR><BR>

');

 FOR parm IN (select name, value from v$parameter
                order by name)
LOOP
  if parm.value is null then
     parm.value := 'null';
  end if;

htp.prn('
  <TR>
  <TD>');
htp.prn( parm.name );
htp.prn('</TD>
  =
  <TD>');
htp.prn( parm.value );
htp.prn('</TD><BR>
  </TR>
');
 END LOOP;
htp.prn('
</BODY>
</HTML>


');
 END;

37 rows selected.
```

The code generated by *loadpsp* looks different than the source that was submitted. The PSP executable has added some extra code into the body of the PSP code. The added code is mainly calls to the *htp* package. This package generates the HTML tags for the web page.

Executing the PSP from SQL*Plus

The PSP can be executed from SQL*Plus, and using the *owa_util* package, the HTML output will be displayed. When accessing the *owa_util* package from SQL*Plus, package variables need to be initialized first, otherwise an error will occur on the first execution. Subsequent executions will work fine, just not the first one. To get around this limitation of the *owa* utilities, add the following code to the *login.sql* script located in the *$ORACLE_HOME/sqlplus/admin* directory.

```
DECLARE
name_arr  OWA.VC_ARR;
value_arr OWA.VC_ARR;
BEGIN
   OWA.INIT_CGI_ENV(0, NAME_ARR, VALUE_ARR);
END;
/
```

Now the PSP execution will be successful on the first attempt:

```
SQL> set serveroutput on
SQL> execute parmlistpsp;

PL/SQL procedure successfully completed.

SQL> execute owa_util.showpage;

<HTML>
<HEAD><TITLE>This is a PSP Page!</TITLE></HEAD>
<BODY>
This is a
list of current database parameters: <BR><BR>
```

```
  <TR>

<TD>O7_DICTIONARY_ACCESSIBILITY</TD>
  =
  <TD>FALSE</TD><BR>
  </TR>


<TR>
  <TD>active_instance_count</TD>
=
  <TD>null</TD><BR>
  </TR>

  <TR>
  <TD>aq_tm_processes</TD>
  =

<TD>1</TD><BR>
  </TR>7

  <TR>
  <TD>archive_lag_target</TD>
  =
...
```

Notice from the output above that the text is pure HTML. Oracle executed our query and formatted the HTML including the data returned from the query. The next step is to access this HTML from a web browser.

Executing the PSP through the Browser

The Oracle9i database includes Apache and JServ as part of its standard installation. The default port is 7778, and the URL to access the main page on the local host machine is:

```
http://localhost:7778/
```

NOTE: On some installations no port is required, just http://localhost.

The *localhost* in the URL above should be replaced with the server name or the IP address of the remote box containing the database to access the web server on another Oracle machine.

The Oracle HTTP Server web page (Figure 8.3) is displayed with many options.

Figure 8.3 – Oracle HTTP Server Main Page

Choose the *mod_plsql* configuration menu or access the URL directly:

```
http://localhost:7778/pls/simpledad/admin_/gateway.htm?schema=sample
```

From the Gateway Configuration Menu, the Gateway Database Access Descriptor Settings is the desired option in order to load the page displayed below in Figure 8.4.

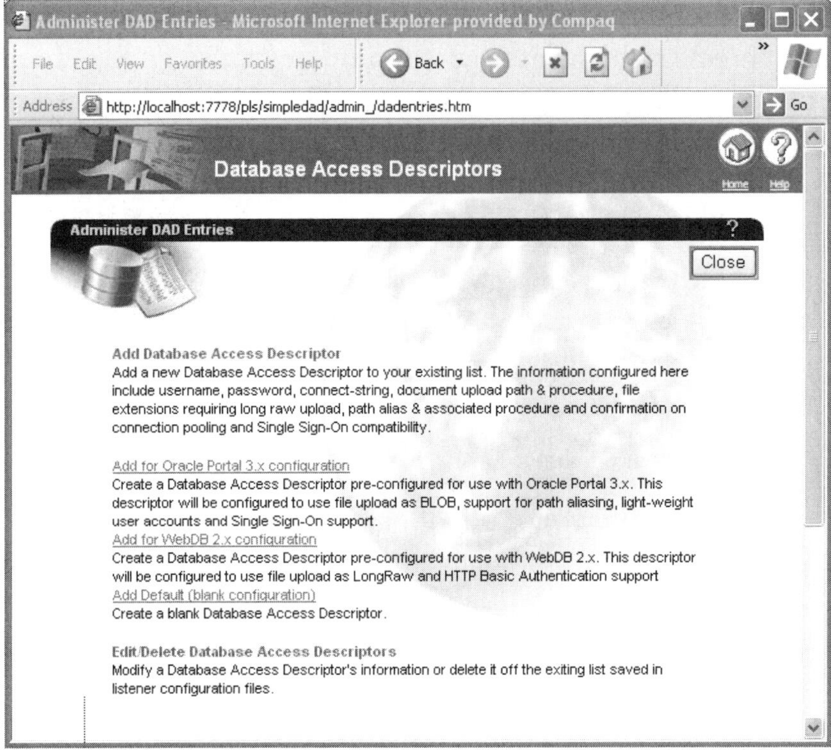

Figure 8.4 – Database Access Descriptors

The Data Access Descriptor (DAD) information is specified on this screen. A DAD simply specifies a username and password to use as the connection to the database. This username and password will be used for anyone that specifies this DAD in their URL specification in the browser. It also supports other optional parameters.

From this screen, a DAD named "test" was created that simply pointed to the local database. Now the PSP is loaded in the database and ready to be accessed. Notice the parts of the URL (http://localhost:7778/pls/test/ParmListPSP) in Figure 8.5:

- **The base URL** - http://localhost:7778
- **PLS** - Fixed text indicating the desired service – PL/SQL.
- **DAD** – The data access descriptor that was created, in this case "test".
- **PSP Name** – The name of the PSP that was loaded into the database.

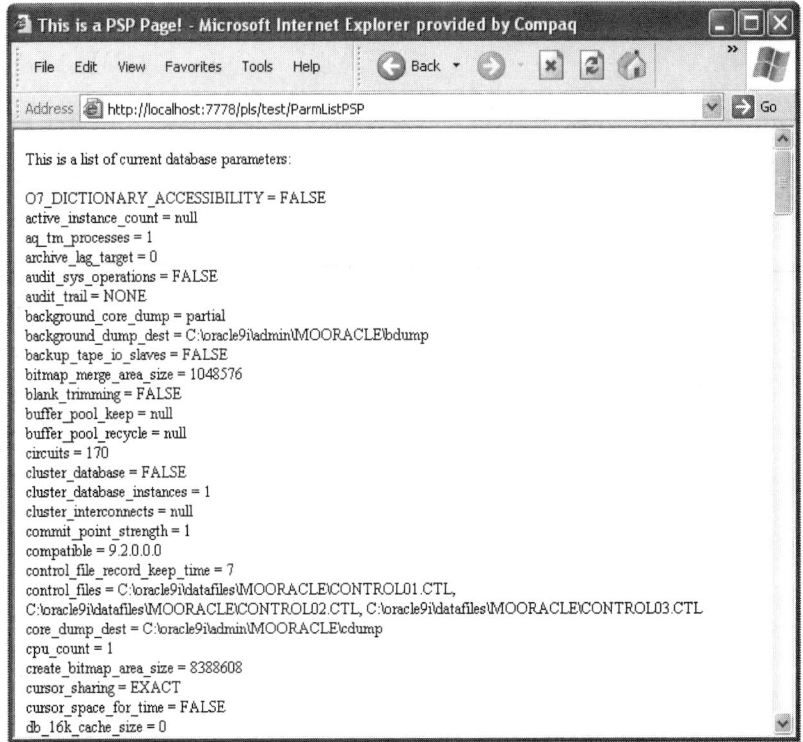
This is a PSP Page! - Microsoft Internet Explorer provided by Compaq
File Edit View Favorites Tools Help
Back
Address http://localhost:7778/pls/test/ParmListPSP
Go
This is a list of current database parameters:
O7_DICTIONARY_ACCESSIBILITY = FALSE
active_instance_count = null
aq_tm_processes = 1
archive_lag_target = 0
audit_sys_operations = FALSE
audit_trail = NONE
background_core_dump = partial
background_dump_dest = C:\oracle9i\admin\MOORACLE\bdump
backup_tape_io_slaves = FALSE
bitmap_merge_area_size = 1048576
blank_trimming = FALSE
buffer_pool_keep = null
buffer_pool_recycle = null
circuits = 170
cluster_database = FALSE
cluster_database_instances = 1
cluster_interconnects = null
commit_point_strength = 1
compatible = 9.2.0.0.0
control_file_record_keep_time = 7
control_files = C:\oracle9i\datafiles\MOORACLE\CONTROL01.CTL,
C:\oracle9i\datafiles\MOORACLE\CONTROL02.CTL, C:\oracle9i\datafiles\MOORACLE\CONTROL03.CTL
core_dump_dest = C:\oracle9i\admin\MOORACLE\cdump
cpu_count = 1
create_bitmap_area_size = 8388608
cursor_sharing = EXACT
cursor_space_for_time = FALSE
db_16k_cache_size = 0

Figure 8.5 – Output Displayed from PSP

Anyone can enter the above URL and the results of the PSP will be displayed in a browser. This simple PSP example queried the database and displayed the instance parameters from the *v$parameter* view in the web page. The sky is the limit for the developer, since any data within Oracle can be easily displayed in a web browser.

Loadpsp Command Line Options

The *loadpsp* executable contains very few command line options. The *replace* option allows the existing procedures in the database to be overlaid regardless of the compilation success. This serves the same purpose as CREATE OR REPLACE when creating PL/SQL objects.

PSPs make it very easy for developers to build Web applications utilizing Oracle built-in technology. PSPs offer the capability of specifying input parameters in HTML and including them in the queries sent to the database. Given the popularity of web-based applications, Oracle developers could utilize PSPs as the foundation for any web solution.

Summary

Oracle provides utilities, such as *loadjava* and *dropjava* that assist developers as well as DBAs. *loadjava* is used to load Java source or class files into the database to be accessed like any other stored program. *dropjava* deletes code loaded by *loadjava*. *loadpsp* provides a way to load a PL/SQL server page into the database and then access it from a browser. SQLJ offers an alternative to JDBC, and the SQLJ executable converts a SQLJ file to a Java file that can be compiled and executed against the database. In addition, developers who want to make their compiled PL/SQL code encrypted and unreadable can employ the *wrap* utility.

Also discussed in this chapter, were the very valuable Oracle supplied packages. *dbms_profiler* provides the only mechanism to benchmark PL/SQL performance on a line-by-line basis. And finally, developers are able to step through stored code by leveraging the *dbms_debug* package, which provides full debugging capability. The utilization of these utilities should not only be encouraged, but required.

Index

V

W

The Oracle In-Focus™ Series

The *Oracle In-Focus*™ series is a unique publishing paradigm, targeted at Oracle professionals who need fast and accurate working examples of complex issues. *Oracle In-Focus*™ books are unique because they have a super-tight focus and quickly provide Oracle professionals with what they need to solve their problems.

Oracle In-Focus™ books are designed for the practicing Oracle professional. Oracle In-Focus™ books are an affordable way for all Oracle professionals to get the information they need, and get it fast.

- **Expert Authors** – All *Oracle In-Focus*™ authors are content experts and are carefully screened for technical ability and communications skills.
- **Online Code Depot** – All code scripts from *Oracle In-Focus*™ are available on the web for instant download. Those who purchase a book will get the URL and password to download their scripts.
- **Lots of working examples** – *Oracle In-Focus*™ is packed with working examples and pragmatic tips.
- **No theory** – Practicing Oracle professionals know the concepts, they need working code to get started fast.
- **Concise** – All *Oracle In-Focus*™ books are less than 200 pages and get right to-the-point of the tough technical issues.
- **Tight focus** - The *Oracle In-Focus*™ series addresses tight topics and targets specific technical areas of Oracle technology.
- **Affordable** – Reasonably priced, *Oracle In-Focus*™ books are the perfect solution to challenging technical issues.

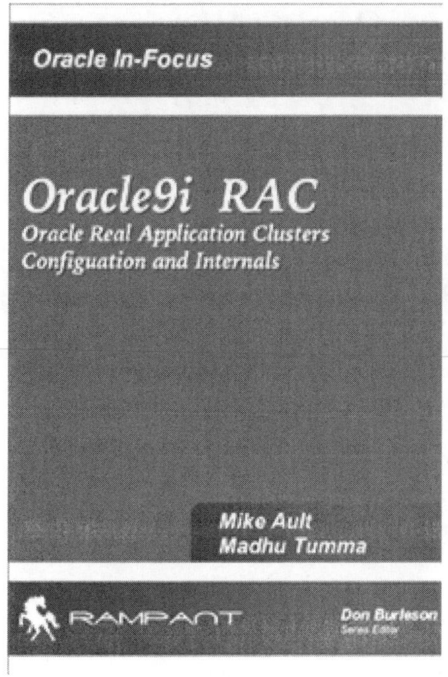

Oracle9i RAC
Oracle Real Application Clusters
Configuration and Internals

Mike Ault & Madhu Tumma
ISBN 0-9727513-0-0
Publication Date - June 2003
Retail Price $59.95 / £37.95

Combining the expertise of two world-renowned RAC experts, Oracle9i RAC is the first-of-its-find reference for RAC and TAF technology. Learn from the experts how to quickly optimizer your Oracle clustered server environment for optimal performance and flexibility.

Covering all areas of RAC continuous availability and transparent application failover, this book is indispensable for any Oracle DBA who is charged with configuring and implementing a RAC clusters database.

Mike Ault is one of the world's most famous Oracle authors with 14 books in-print, and Madhu Tumma is a recognized RAC clustering consultant. Together, Ault and Tumma dive deep inside RAC and show you the secrets for quickly implementing and tuning Oracle9i RAC database systems.

http://www.rampant.cc/

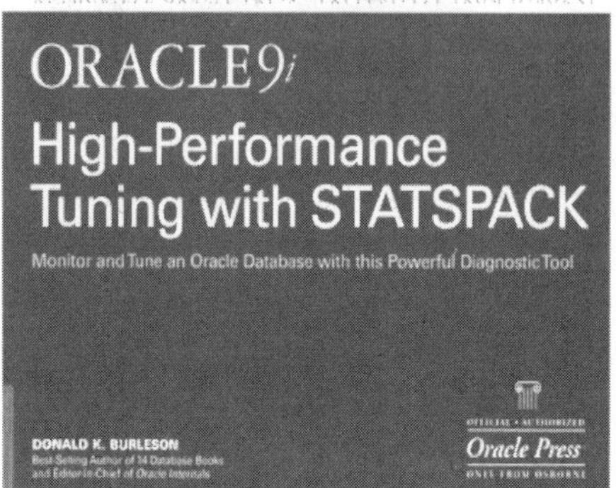

Oracle9i High-Performance Tuning with STATSPACK

Donald Burleson
Oracle Press, Feb 2002
Publisher: McGraw-Hill Osborne Media;
March 22, 2002
ISBN: 007222360X
Copyright: 2001
Retail Price $49.99 US

Get complete coverage of STATSPACK--Oracle's powerful tuning tool--inside this official guide. Including ready-to-use STATSPACK scripts you'll be able to collect and analyze system data and soon have your Oracle database running at peak performance.